Puppy Training Guide

By James J Jackson

The Ultimate Handbook To Train Your Puppy In Obedience, Crate Training, And Potty Training

4th Edition

Puppy Training Guide 4th Edition

Table of Contents

Introduction

I want to thank you and congratulate you for purchasing the book, *"Puppy Training Guide: The Ultimate handbook to train your puppy in obedience, crate training and potty training"*.

This exclusive eBook for puppy owners will teach you the fundamentals of obedience training, crate training and potty training. There are outlined pointers that will introduce you to the very essence of training your puppy. In addition, the guidelines that you will find within this book will enable you to have full control over your puppy through proper commands. This will also teach you how to properly motivate your puppy in times of accidents and discouragement.

In this book, only the most efficient, effective, and stress-free strategies are given in order to give the reader the best value for his money. As such, it is only fitting that only the major issues and problems that may arise as a result of obedience, crate, and potty training are thoroughly discussed.

By consistently practicing the strategies outlined in this book, the author is very confident that you will be able to properly train your puppy without putting it into unnecessary stress and suffering.

Remember that a well-trained puppy is a well-behaved pet – one that will create a better relationship between the puppy and the owner. A better relationship between the pet and the owner makes a happy household. Always remember to take care of your puppy and be patient with its learning curve. Happy training!

Thanks again for purchasing this book, I hope you enjoy it!

Chapter 1 - The Fundamentals of Puppy Training

In this chapter, you will learn:

1. The Purpose Of Puppy Training
2. How To Use Voice Tones In Training Your Puppy
3. How To Use Body Language In Training Your Puppy
4. The Fundamentals Of Mental Leash Control
5. The Fundamentals Of Temper Tantrums
6. Metal Link Slip Collar
7. Equipment You Need To Train Your Puppy
8. Durations of Training
9. Managing your puppy's behavior
10. Puppy Socialization
11. Puppy socialization and vaccination

The Purpose of Puppy Training

Most dog and puppy training principles in the past were dependent on tyrannical methods in order to train pet puppies. In other words, the negative reinforcement strategy was widely used. As such, there are a lot of puppy owners out there who have difficulty implementing the right principles in training their puppies. This is because they are constantly worrying that their puppies might not be able to withstand coercive training strategies. Because of this, many owners of puppies avoid training altogether until their puppies become adult dogs. In other words, there was a lot of valuable time that is wasted from the moment a puppy is born until it becomes an adult dog.

However, in recent years, there was a shift in the field of dog and puppy training. People started to use positive reinforcement in their dog and puppy training efforts. As such, there was a revolution in this field. Many experts in canine behavior started to experiment with lure-reward techniques in order to control their dogs and puppies.

At this point of time, both positive and negative reinforcement strategies are widely used. This is because experts believe that using one strategy at the expense of the other is not effective at all. As such, throughout this book, you will be learning how to use both positive and negative reinforcement.

Basically, you can teach a lot to your puppy as long as you remain consistent. What you need to understand is consistent training with the correct strategies is the best means of effectively training your puppy. Listed below are some of the benefits that you will enjoy in training your puppy:

Effective puppy training methods will enable your puppy to have good behavior, manners and obedience before he or she forms bad behavior and becomes unruly as is his or her nature.

- Your puppy will learn to behave and act normally in different situations and environments that involve interaction with the following:
  - Other dogs
  - Other animals

- o Different people in the household
- o Different people outside the household
- Effective puppy training methods will enable your puppy to have advanced brain development. This in turn will be beneficial for you because you will have an easier time in teaching him or her more difficult tricks in the near future.
- Your puppy won't develop bad manners such as biting and/or barking at other people or jumping around the house to the detriment of your valuable (i.e. breakable) possessions.

 The main purpose of training your puppy is to enable you to have a puppy that is behaved. In addition, you also want to have a dog that listens to you and have the capability to follow your commands. Remember to first teach basic commands first before moving on to more complex commands and instructions. The puppy is like an infant. As such, it cannot learn everything overnight. Therefore, exercise patience when your puppy is just starting to learn.

You can do this by consistently training your puppy correctly. This is because when you start to train your dog when it is already an adult, it may no longer follow commands. Remember the saying that old dogs cannot learn new tricks? That is mostly true. Therefore, it would be very beneficial if you start to correctly train your puppy right from the start.

How to Use Voice Tones in Training Your Puppy

There are three basic voice tones that you can use in order to correctly train your puppy. These tones are the following:

1. Praising voice tone
2. Commanding voice tone
3. Corrective voice tone

The first (Praising voice tone) refers to the tone that you use in order to express appreciation to your puppy. In addition, praising voice tone also refers to that you use in order to encourage your puppy for a job well done. The perfect examples of praises are the words, "Good dog!" or "Good puppy!"

The second one (Commanding voice tone) refers to one you use in a way that is 'matter of fact.' Hence, this tone is very direct to the puppy.

For the puppy, this is an indication that you mean business, you are serious in your command, and that he must follow the command accordingly. Take note however, that the commanding voice tone has absolutely nothing to do with shouting at your puppy. Nothing could be further from the truth. In fact, if you do shout at your puppy, it will most likely have an adverse effect on him. Later on, the puppy may become a dog that does not want to interact with people and other dogs because of fear and trauma.

If your puppy is by nature respectful and submissive, you will have an easier time accomplishing the training sessions. However, most of the time, puppies are

not submissive, and there will definitely be struggles.

Hence, there are cases where your puppy does not consider you as his or her master – at least not yet. If you are not successful in establishing your authority and master position over your puppy, you will notice the following:

- Your puppy will often bite your hands
- Your puppy will bark at you a lot
- Your puppy growls quite a lot
- Your puppy constantly bites and pulls on your clothes
- Your puppy struggles to get up when asked to
- Your puppy is nipping
- Your puppy shows his or her teeth when you are trying to command him or her.

If you notice the signs mentioned above, you need to remind your puppy that you are his or her master and not the other way around. What you can do is to tell him or her with a firm, commanding voice the word, "No!" whenever your puppy manifests any of these signs.

The third one (Corrective voice tone) refers to the tone that you use in order to make the puppy know that what he is doing is not correct, and is not to be permitted. You can do this by saying a firm, hard "No." For the puppy, this indicates that you are serious and are displeased that what he just did cannot be permitted and must not be done again. Do not always do this corrective tone for a puppy because most puppies are sensitive. Use them only for behaviors that clearly cannot be permitted.

How to Use Body Language in Training Your Puppy

 True, the use of different voice tones in training your puppy is a crucial component in its learning. However, remember that body language is also a crucial factor in the development of your puppy. In fact, you can use body language in order to teach him more efficiently. As an illustrative example, you can use certain hand and body signals from the moment the puppy was born. In this way, the puppy will easily learn it. As such, the certain hand and body signals will be inculcated to the puppy until he becomes a full-grown dog. In addition, you can also use motions and positions that are subtle to help your puppy understand your commands more easily. In this way, the puppy can easily relate to what you are trying to say.

The Fundamentals of Mental Leash Control

Mental leash control happens when you can fully control your puppy while he is still thinking about doing something. In other words, you will anticipate your puppy's actions while he is thinking about doing something (for example, running towards a table or floor).

Simply stated, mental leash control means that you constantly practice the skill of being able to anticipate or read the actions of your puppy and being able to respond in a way that is efficient. As an illustrative example, if your puppy is trying to run towards a table and you have anticipated it, what you can do is to grab him so that he will not be able to run. Once you are able to master the signs when your puppy is going to do something; that is where the fun and excitement of becoming a puppy owner starts.

The Fundamentals of Temper Tantrums

There will be times that your puppy will throw a temper tantrum. The truth of the matter is that some temper tantrums can still be present even if the puppy becomes an adult dog. However, what you can do is to recognize these temper tantrums in order to lessen it somewhat. In this way, this behavior of your puppy will be stopped from the very beginning so that he will lose this behavior once he becomes an adult dog.

The only way to recognize the puppy temper tantrums is through observation. Remember that temper tantrums come in many forms and are  dependent on the personality of your puppy. Remember that the temper tantrums are not something that is inherently bad. The truth is, it is just a reflex for your puppy for feeling frustrated or confused in something.

There are four basic types of puppy personalities that you can observe in your dog:

1. The prey puppy personality– the temper tantrum of this type of personality is a high pitch whining or screaming sound
2. The pack puppy personality – the temper tantrum of this type of personality is sulking sound
3. The fight puppy personality – the temper tantrum of this type of personality is grumble or growl
4. The flight puppy personality – the temper tantrum of this type of personality is by crawling into a submissive posture

Metal Link Slip Collar

The metal link slip collar is an essential tool you can use in order to control your puppy. This is especially true when you bring your puppy to environments, places and situations where there are a lot of distractions such as parks, malls and family gatherings. Remember that this collar is not to restrain or to hurt your puppy. Instead, the purpose of the metal link slip collar is to train your puppy so that he will behave in the situations that have been mentioned above.

How to use the metal link slip collar:

Step 1: Stretch the metal link slip collar

Step 2: Hold the rings

Step 3: Hold your puppy's head

Step 4: Slip the collar into your puppy's head

Note: When intending to purchase a metal link slip collar, do not buy the choke chain type. This is not recommended because this type of collar has been observed to damage the esophagus of dogs and puppies. As such, choke chain type of collars is dangerous and harmful to your puppy.

Equipment You Need To Train Your Puppy

Prepare the following pieces of equipment that you can use to train your puppy:

- 20 to 30 foot rope that is made from lightweight materials such as nylon and cotton
    a. This rope will be used when you intend to train your puppy in distances.

- A basic leash that is 6 foot long
    - b. This basic leash will be used to train your puppy around the house, during obedience training, crate training, and potty training of your puppy

Durations of Training

In essence, the duration of your puppy training is dependent on your specific work schedule, free time and lifestyle. As such, the duration of training will differ from one person to another. If you are a person who works throughout the day, the best way to train your puppy is to do it after you come home from work.

This means that, given your schedule, the best time you can train your puppy is at night. Take note that what is important in training your puppy is the consistency (yours and your puppy's) in following the program. As such, you have to make sure your puppy is able to master the first step before going to the second.

After several weeks of consistent training, you will be amazed by the benefits of training your puppy. This means that over that span of time, you will notice that your puppy becomes educated and can therefore be easily controlled. For example, you can train your puppy every day, every other day or at least thrice a week.

 Take note, however, that different puppies respond to training differently

– some puppies will learn fast and some puppies will learn slowly. This is because different breeds of dogs are by nature fast learners while other breeds are not. For example, puppies which are from the terrier breeds, border collie breeds, and Siberian husky breeds take a longer time to learn new things. As such, it would be important to be patient with your puppy. Persist in training him or her! In this respect, remember the principle that "persistence removes resistance."

Managing your puppy's behavior

Puppies have behaviors that are instilled in them by nature. This includes the following:
- Eating and ingesting any small object they see around the house
- Chewing on any object they see around the house
- Urinating anywhere whenever they feel the need to do so
- Defecating anywhere whenever they feel the need to do so
- Barking whenever they realize they are alone
- Whining
- Becoming unruly
- Crying for no reason
- Biting everything
- Biting everyone
- Jumping up and down whenever they are excited

What you need to remember is that all the aforementioned behaviors are normal for puppies and also adult dogs that grew up untrained. In addition, you may have noticed that many of these behaviors are definitely characteristics that no one would like in a dog. The only way to get rid of these behaviors is to train your puppy the right way. Listed below are quick tips and tricks in managing your puppy's behaviors:

1. Whenever your puppy is becoming unruly, confine and isolate him or her in a single area in your home such as the bedroom or the kitchen.

2. You have to remember that constant supervision of your puppy is the key to correctly training him or her. The reason for this is that training an adult dog is no longer as effective. In other words, it is best to start training your puppy while he or she is still young. Otherwise, you will have a hard time supervising your pet.

3. Never forget to praise, reward, and pat your puppy on the head (positive reinforcement for your pet) whenever he or she exhibits good behavior. This will significantly improve the degree of communication with your puppy.

4. Conversely, do not praise, reward and pat your puppy on the head (negative reinforcement for your pet) whenever he or she exhibits bad behavior.

5. It is a good idea to train your puppy to become well-behaved whenever you are not present. This means that you will teach him that you will not be around most of the time. How can you do this?

- Whenever your puppy is left alone and upon your return, your puppy whines, cries and barks at you, DO NOT provide him or her with positive reinforcement. This will give your puppy the idea that you can be manipulated and that crying, barking, and whining are effective means of getting your attention.
- Another thing you can do is to leave the room a lot of times during the day in very short period of time (3 minutes). You should do this act casually. Once you are able to accomplish this, your puppy will get used to not being by your side all the time.

6. Puppies have a lot of energy in their body. What you can do to manage their behavior is to burn this energy up. You can do this by performing the obedience exercises discussed in Chapter 2. Also, you can accompany your puppy outside the house and let him or her walk around, run around, and even play with other puppies or dogs. In addition, you can also learn advanced dog tricks that include the following:
   - Hide and seek
   - Playing fetch
   - Tugging
   - Catching frisbees
   - Fly-the-ball game

7. If your present job requires you to put in long hours and thus diminish your quality time with your puppy, it might be prudent to avail of the services of a pet daycare center or a pet nanny.

Puppy Socialization

The best time to train your puppy to socialize with other people, other puppies/dogs and other animals is between the ages of 4 and 14 weeks. In this way, the bonds that are formed  between your puppy and others will last him or her a lifetime. In other words, you should take advantage of the 4 to 14 week window to let your puppy socialize. Otherwise, your puppy will suffer. According to a recent research conducted by experts on animal behavior, puppies that were not socialized sufficiently between the ages of 4 and 14 weeks with other people, dogs/puppies and animals will have aggression and fear problems and issues when they become adult dogs.

In light of this finding, you must exert effort in introducing your puppy to different experiences with other people and animals. However, remember that your puppy must be properly vaccinated before such introductions. Some of the best places where you can bring your puppy for purposes of socialization are malls, public parks, and even supermarkets.

By and large, cats and dogs have aggression issues. If you have both cats and dogs as your family pets, it will be beneficial if you teach them how to live with each other without fighting. What you can do is to introduce your puppy to the family cat. In this way, your puppy will grow up not hating cats in general.

Besides other animals and other people, it is also important to introduce your puppy to different things. The reason for this is that puppies by nature make mental notes of new objects that they learned or encountered. In this way, they will not behave badly once they encounter something or someone new. How do you execute this? You can simply bring your puppy in the living room while you are watching TV. In addition, you can also bring your puppy in the kitchen while you are cooking. Also, you can introduce your puppy to your car so that he or she will get used to noises in the streets, pedestrians crossing, the environment, and the weather.

It will also help if you will avoid introducing your puppy to negative situations. An example of a negative situation is fighting between family members.

Listed below is a quick guide on the people, animals, places, and objects that you should introduce your puppy to between the ages of 4 and 14 weeks:

1. Persons
    - Infants
    - Toddlers
    - juniors
    - teenagers
    - young adults
    - adults (middle aged)
    - adults (seniors)
    - people with disabilities
    - people that are uniformed

- people that are loud
- people that are silent and reserved
- a person that wears gloves
- a person that wears a hat
- a person that wears a helmet
- a person that wears a beard
- a person that wears glasses
- a person with an umbrella

2. Animals
    - Puppies of different breeds
    - Puppies of the same breed
    - Adult dogs of different breeds
    - Adult dogs of the same breed
    - Horses
    - Stags
    - Pigs
    - Chickens
    - Kittens/Cats
    - Pet birds like parrots and canaries

3. Places
    - Parks
    - Veterinary clinic
    - Dog salon
    - Shopping malls
    - Parties
    - Club/bar
    - Church (if permissible)
    - Schoolyards
    - Backyard

- Garage
- Inside the car
- Busy street (while walking)
- Floors that are slippery
- Slopes and hills

4. Vehicles/Modes of Transport

- Motorcycle
- Rollerblades
- Bicycle
- Shopping cart (in the grocery store or supermarket)
- Trucks
- Skateboards
- Bus

Chapter 2 – The Ultimate Guide to Teaching Respect

Teaching respect and gaining the puppy's trust is the most fundamental thing any owner or trainer must do. A puppy who knows how to respect his owner is a well-behaved, well-adjusted, good-tempered dog. Teaching your puppy anything is easier when he trusts and respects you. Obedience training, potty training, and all the tricks are easily learned by a puppy who respects his master.

Why respect is important

Respect is the basis for developing a mutually satisfying relationship between you and your dog. It is also the fundamental building block of having good and effective communication between you two.

Respect for the owner is very important because it is a sign that your puppy recognizes you as his pack leader. Dogs are pack animals and they need to belong to a pack in order to live well. And packs always have rules which are enforced by a pack leader. The leader occupies the alpha position in the pack. He is responsible for keeping the entire pack in line. He is the one who makes all the decisions. It is crucial for you to establish that the alpha position belongs to you alone. Without this, you will likely have an unruly and misbehaving dog in your hands.

Your puppy's pack consists of you and your family. And the alpha position belongs to you. If you do not take this leadership position, your puppy will naturally take the alpha position. Soon, he will rule over you, your family, and other dogs or pets in the house. This is not something you would want because having your puppy as the alpha is a recipe for disaster. Your puppy will become a burden rather than an adorable, obedient, and good-mannered pet.

Signs that your puppy is not respecting you

Most owners do not immediately establish the leadership position with their new puppy. Soon, the puppy grows up not respecting their owners and turning into the dominant or alpha dog. Here are the common signs that show your puppy is not respecting you:

- Too much barking

  Barking is your puppy's way of establishing an alpha position over the entire household. It may also be a sign of defiance to your authority. Often, dominant dogs will bark a lot when there are other people in the house or when you and your family are all in the same room. This is his way of imposing his voice over everyone else. It's kind of like shouting at everyone "I'm the boss here! You all listen to me!"

- Getting on the bed or the furniture anytime he feels like it, without any permission

  Beds and furniture are your possessions, your territory. If your puppy gets on either of these without waiting for your permission, it is his way of putting you in the subordinate position. He is deliberately encroaching on your personal space because he feels he is the alpha and he can pretty much go to wherever he wants or do whatever he wants. This lack of respect for personal space is a clear sign he is establishing his dominance over you.

- Growling at people, even at you

  Growling is a natural behavior that a dog uses to warn others. It's like saying "Get back. I don't like your behavior and I will bite you if you don't stay back." When a dog growls, a bite is just a few moments away.

  This behavior is also a display of dominance, a way of marking territory, or a sign he is displeased with you. These behaviors indicate that your puppy is establishing dominance over others. If he does this growling thing with you, it is clear he is warning you to stay in line or else.

- Frequently demands attention by mouthing, whining or nudging

  It's fun when your puppy seeks your attention. What isn't fun is when it is constant and your puppy becomes very demanding. Hours of whining, mouthing, and nudging are more of a nuisance than a fun activity with your puppy. These behaviors mean that your puppy is establishing dominance over you. He is trying to force you to pay attention to him whenever he wants you to.

- Guarding behavior over toys or food

  In the wild, dogs fiercely guard their territories. This is basically a function of the alpha. In your home, guarding behavior should not be observed. You are the pack leader and you are expected to do the protecting. If your puppy growls at you when you approach his food or toys, it is an indication that he is trying to exert his dominance over you. He does not see you as his leader; rather, he sees you as a subordinate who is trying to encroach on his space. He is also trying to show you that he does not have to follow your orders.

- Refusing to move out of the way

  If your puppy refuses to move out of the doorway or when he deliberately blocks your path despite your orders, it is a sign of dominance. He is challenging your authority. He feels he does not have to follow you because you are not his recognized pack leader. It shows he does not respect you.

- Refuse to be handled

  Your puppy's refusal to allow anyone to handle him is a display of dominance. This means everyone, not even you or the vet. The behavior is an indication that your puppy does not respect humans.

- Humping

  This is very embarrassing. It is really bad manners when guests arrive in your home and your puppy makes a beeline to their legs and starts humping. This behavior displays dominance. In the wild, dogs only hump other animals that they deem as inferior to them. If he does this to you or other people, it is an indication that he is trying to subjugate everyone who enters his territory.

- Ignoring the commands that he has already learned

  Willful disregard of commands is a sign of disrespecting authority, particularly if the commands are those he has already learned. He feels he doesn't have to obey you because he sees you as his subordinate.

- Poop or pee on furniture or your bed

  Your possessions, especially your bed, are your territories. Your bed is your most personal space. When your puppy pees or poops on it, it is a deliberate, blatant display of disrespecting your authority. This indicates how low he regards your authority because he sees himself as superior to you.

Why you should be the alpha

Dogs need to belong to a pack in order for them to live well. Upon birth, a puppy's pack is the litter he belongs to. The alpha is his mother. In this pack, all the puppy's needs are provided for by the alpha (his mother). His mother feeds him, protects him, and comforts him. His socialization is with the rest of the litter. Once the puppy is removed from his litter, he loses his pack. If left alone, a dog becomes aggressive, unruly and untamed. You and your family, and any pets you already have, become your puppy's pack once you bring him home with you.

When your puppy enters your pack, you should establish that you are the alpha. If there is no alpha, the puppy's natural instincts would prompt him to fill in this role. One mistake that most owners make is that they assume that their puppies would automatically recognize them (the owners) as the leaders. They assume that since they are humans, they are automatically regarded as superior. They believe that they do not have to make any effort to assert their leadership.

Puppies need to go through a process called subordination in order to be established within a pack. They need to know the pack dynamics, the rules they need to follow, who the alpha is, and what their place is within the pack. The process of subordination starts by the 3rd week of a puppy's life and continues all throughout the puppy's early development stage. During this time, it is natural for puppies to push boundaries and challenge authority. It is therefore crucial for puppies to be consistently reminded of pack rules and hierarchy.

There are steps that every owner should take in order to establish pack leadership. When they establish their alpha position, it will be much easier to communicate with their puppies and establish respect.

How to be the alpha

Subordination is taught very early in a puppy's life. It starts with the mother. She grabs the puppy's neck. In a firm and gentle hold, she pins the puppy to the ground. This establishes that she is the alpha and that the puppy is a subordinate. She does this repeatedly, especially when the puppy behaves out of line. Once leadership has been established, the puppy will show signs of respect. The puppy would approach his mother in a nearly crouching stance. He approaches slowly and then nuzzles his mother's neck and nose.

For humans, establishing the alpha position is different. The basic steps include practicing the alpha exercises and stance. You also have to create, control and maintain pack activities.

Alpha exercises- These are also called leadership exercises. These help to establish that you, as the owner, are the head of the pack. Once this is established, your puppy will seek you out. He will desire spending time with you. He will also treat you with affection and respect. It will also be easier to communicate with, handle, and teach your dog.

The following exercises will help you in establishing your alpha position. However, these steps are not recommended for puppies that have already learned how to use their teeth. In other words, these exercises are not recommended for puppies that have already learned to bite. The 1ˢᵗ 2 exercises are most applicable for 3-month old puppies. The 3rd and 4th exercises are most applicable for puppies not older than 6 months and do not display any aggressive behaviors yet. In all the following the following exercises, be firm but gentle. Treat your puppies as you would a human baby.

> **Exercise 1**- Call or go near your puppy and sit beside him. Pick him up, holding him just under his front legs. He should be facing you. The 4 fingers of both your hands should be supporting behind the front legs. Both of your thumbs should be over his chest. Hold him at arm's length away from you, at eye level. Look at him directly in the eyes. If your puppy struggles, make growling noises at him. Make some guttural sounds and keep holding him until you see him relax. Hold your puppy in this position several times a day, for about 15-45 seconds each time. Vary the length of time you hold him this way. Also, vary the times you do this and where.

> **Exercise 2**- Sit down on the floor, next or in front of your puppy. Hold your puppy upside down. Put one of your hands and rest it under your puppy's head. This will support his head while he hangs. Use your other hand to support his back. Your hands will be fully supporting his entire body. For a larger puppy, hold him in this same position but rest him on his back across your lap. Keep your puppy in this position for 15-45 seconds. If he struggles while you hold him, create low sounds from your throat. You growling is meant to keep him still, a command to keep himself in the position you placed him in. once the puppy relaxes, slowly and gently release him.

> **Exercise 3**- For larger puppies, this exercise should be used instead of the first 2. Start by straddling your

puppy while he lies on his stomach on the floor. You should be on top of his back. Place one leg on each of the puppy's side. You and your puppy should be facing in the same direction. Hold your puppy a little behind his front legs. Place your hands under your puppy's chest and lock your fingers. Lift him off the floor for 15-45 seconds. Make growling noises at him if he struggles.

Exercise 4- Position your puppy on all fours on the floor with his legs should be pointing away from you. With one hand on his neck, hold your puppy firmly. Press down gently but firmly on the midsection using your other hand. Start talking to him in a soft voice. Continue until he quiets down and you feel his body relaxing. This may take about 2 to 3 minutes. While in this position, do not let him to nip, get up or struggle. Keep him steady. If your puppy starts to expose his belly for a belly rub, this means you are succeeding. This may take a few sessions, though. Always provide him generous amounts of praise in a soft and quiet voice once you feel him relax in your hands. Then, hold all 4 of his legs. Look at his mouth briefly so that he will be accustomed to handling. Do this exercise 4 to 5 times each day. Reduce the frequency of this exercise as your puppy gets more used to your handling and starts to accept you as his pack leader.

Stare exercise- The stare or eye contact is a crucial part of determining who is superior. In a pack, only the alpha is allowed to use "the stare". It is used to keep order within the pack. It is also a reminder of who is in charge. You should use this to express that you are the pack leader.

Start by making eye contact with your puppy and maintain it for a few seconds. Make this a pleasant experience for your puppy. Look at him directly in the eye in a neutral way. No frowning, scrunching your eyebrows, or looking angry. Also, do not force your puppy to maintain or make eye contact. Get him to look at you with simple commands like "Look at me" or "watch me". Follow his line of sight and get him to look you in the eye. The moment you two make eye contact, give generous amounts of praise. This may take some time.

Most importantly, never use "The Stare" with a puppy who has already established dominance. A puppy who already thinks of himself as the one in charge would make eye contact but won't be willing to avert his eyes first. You will be locked in a staring game where you have a huge possibility of losing. If you look away or even slightly blink first, you are just confirming him his alpha status. This exercise will work more for him than for you. In this case, you should try other leadership exercises first before you do "The Stare". Practice other activities where you teach him to recognize and accept you as his leader before attempting this exercise.

Exercising your alpha status

Establishing your alpha status is one thing; maintaining it is another. As the alpha, you should initiate activities where you re-affirm your pack leader status. Incorporate these activities in your dog's daily routine. You can also include these in your puppy's training schedule for each day.

The most important command that reminds your puppy of your leadership is the "Sit" command. It keeps him reminded that you are the one in charge. Include this in everyday activities. For example, tell him to sit before you place his food in front of him. Do not feed him unless he sits. This shows that you will provide for his basic needs if he obeys you. Give the "sit" command before you play or before going out the door. This also shows him that he must obey your orders in order to obtain permission to indulge in activities that he finds pleasurable.

Your leadership is more readily accepted if your demands are fair and consistent. Never allow your puppy to snap or growl. Give him a severe shake at the scruff (the loose skin that surrounds the neck of your puppy) and avoid giving him any attention for 10-15 minutes. If you are already comfortable handling him, take him by the scruff of the neck with both of your hands, look directly at his eyes and give him a firm shake. Put him down in the crate and leave him there for 15 to 20 minutes. Do not give him any attention during this time. Be consistent because a single incident that you did not properly address will offset all the hard work you did to establish your alpha position.

If you are afraid when your puppy snaps or growls at you, it is best to seek professional help. Approaching an aggressive dog when you are nervous or afraid is more likely to set him off. You won't be controlling him effectively in this state. He will sense your nervousness and become more aggressive. It may even result to biting. A dog who is allowed to threaten members of his pack is likely to become a biter. When your puppy snaps or growls at you or any other member of the family, take him to seek professional help. Do not ignore this kind of behavior.

It is also very important never to ignore any behavior that challenges your authority. Be consistent in keeping your puppy in line. There will be times when dogs challenge their owner's leadership. This is especially so when the puppy reaches adolescence. Respond to these behaviors immediately. For example, your dog does not follow your commands. Give him the "stare" and a firm shake then give the command again. Most often, he would resume his obedient state after this.

How to be an effective pack leader

To be an effective pack leader, be consistent in maintaining order. Whenever your puppy behaves out of line, address it immediately. Even if you are tired or not feeling up to it, give him a firm shake, look him directly in the eye, and say "No" or "Stop". Put him down in a corner or crate and ignore him for 15 to 20 minutes. If you fail to give a timely and adequate response when he misbehaves, he will continue misbehaving. You will soon find yourself living with an aggressive, unruly dog. Your puppy will challenge your leadership and try to usurp the alpha position from you.

Confidence and Assertiveness. A pack leader should always exude a confident and assertive energy. Rules are enforced in a quiet but firm manner. Take your cue from a mother dog. Whenever a puppy strays away from the den, she calmly picks him up by the scruff of the neck and puts him back to his place in the litter. She never misses to do this. As a result, her puppies respect her leadership and follow her around obediently.

Whenever you deal with your dog, be calm and assertive. This is most important when he growls, snaps or misbehaves. Never approach your dog when you are nervous or emotional. Your energy influences your puppy's behavior. He will feel this energy and will make him nervous, too. Nervous dogs turn aggressive. They become overprotective of you. They feel the need to step up, take the leadership position, and protect you from whatever is making you nervous.

Territories are also very important. A pack leader should be able to assert ownership over a territory and defend it well. In the wild, the pack leader claims a space for the entire pack and guards it well. Anyone who strays into pack space is immediately dealt with, either by a warning growl or a fatal bite. You should also make it clear to your puppy that he lives in your territory and that he should respect your domain. Establish ownership over your territory (i.e., house/apartment, etc.) by using clear body language and eye contact. It will be easy to teach your puppy where he can pee/poo, where to eat, and not to climb on the furniture/bed if he sees you as his pack leader. He will learn to respect the space you own.

Waiting. This is another way to assert your leadership. It is a psychological exercise of maintaining your alpha position. Puppies under their mother's leadership have to wait before they can feed. In the wild, adult dogs have to wait for their alpha's permission before they can leave to hunt, play or explore. In your home, you should also teach your puppy to wait. You have to keep addressing their instinctual need for directions. They are also naturally inclined to wait and work in order to get food. Your puppy no longer needs to hunt to have something to eat but you can still make him work to get it. You can do this by taking him out for a walk before you serve him his food. Wait until he calms down and becomes submissive. The walk should help your puppy achieve this state, especially if he is energetic.

Know your pack. This is the defining quality of a good pack leader. Know the needs of your pack and address in a timely and satisfactory manner. Learn to read the signals your puppy is sending you. Know when he is sick, afraid, stressed, energetic, hurt or hungry. When you promptly address your puppy's needs, he learns to trust and depend on you. You should also learn how to set a schedule for your puppy, with each activity having definite set of goals. You should commit to these goals and follow through with each activity.

This way, you strengthen the bond between you and your puppy. You also develop a deeper and more meaningful relationship for both of you.

A true pack leader should be balanced (giving discipline and love, needs and pleasure), honest, real and present. Here are more things to remember in order to be an effective and respected leader of the pack:

- It is very important to match the dog breed to your lifestyle. Do not get a large hunting breed if you have very limited space (e.g., living in an apartment or condo unit). Do not get a dog breed that requires more frequent exercises if you are likely to keep him inside the home for long periods. Do not get a dog that requires a lot of attention and play time if you will be away from him most of the time.

- Involve the rest of the family in the care of your puppy. Give each person a role and responsibility before you bring the puppy home. This way, your puppy sees that his new pack is well organized with each member having specific roles and responsibilities. It will be much easier for him to settle down to his own role as well. This will also show how well you manage the pack.

- Arrange a carefully balanced daily schedule. You should incorporate exercise, training and play to improve your puppy's physical and mental health. The best way to provide for all these is going for a power walk. Take your dog outside and walk for about 30-45 minutes. The walk exercises his body, as well as releasing mental energy. It is also a pleasurable activity as he gets to address his instinctive love for the outdoors.

- Designate certain times in each day for mental exercises. These exercises include maintaining and reinforcing the rules, limitations and boundaries. As your puppy satisfactorily achieves each task, give him appropriate praise. Your affections are already a form of reward for your puppy.

- Whatever you do or wherever you go, always be in front of your dog. Do not allow him to pull you along. The alpha dog is the leader, and that means both figuratively and literally. When you are out for a walk, walk in front of him. He can be allowed to walk or trot beside you but never even a step ahead. When you pass through doorways, pass through first. Never give your dog an opportunity to get ahead of you.

- Before you give your puppy affection, a toy, food, or water, have him obey a command first. Tell him to sit or stay. This way, he will consider food, toys, etc. as rewards for his good behavior and not a right.

How to teach respect to your puppy

Once you have established your alpha position in the pack, it is now time to teach your puppy to respect you. Your alpha position is crucial for him to look up to you and know that what you say should be followed.

Make sure to give your puppy appropriate praise. He loves to please and wants to get positive attention from you. Provide both whenever he displays good behavior.

Remember to be always consistent whether displaying pack leader behavior or giving praise. This way, your puppy will know what to expect when he behaves a certain way. This will also prevent any confusion and help in training him faster.

Be gentle and kind but remain firm. Avoid giving harsh punishments such as hitting or yelling. Otherwise, your puppy will fear you instead of respect you.

Make him a real member of your family. For your puppy, you and your family are his new family. He does not see any substantial difference between you and his litter (well, of course except for the human forms). Treat him like that, too. Get the entire family involved. Encourage them to treat your puppy as a real member and be consistent with how they treat him.

Play with your puppy. This achieves 2 things: exercise and bonding. Exercise is very important in a dog's life. It strengthens his body and improves his mental health. His energies are released in an acceptable manner, helping him behave better. Playing with your dog also strengthens the bond between you two. It helps him to get to know you and your family, also and solidify your pack.

Provide adequate care. Make sure to address his needs like food and shelter. His needs also include attention and love. As a good pack leader, you should be able to provide all these. This way, your puppy knows that everything he needs, he can get from you. He will respect you for that.

Be fair. Treat all pets in your home equally. If your puppy senses you treat him better than the other pets, he will likely feel more important and be less obedient and respectful. If your puppy feels left out, he will feel he has to fight harder for your attention and become an aggressive dog.

Signs that your puppy respects you

Respect has nothing to do with your puppy's loyalty, though. Dogs are always loyal to their owners and will do everything to protect them. He may guard you, your family and your home adequately but it does not mean he respects your authority. Respect is observed in the way your puppy interacts with you.

Happiness- An indication that your puppy respects you is when he is happy to see you. He is happy when he wags his tail enthusiastically, with a submissive body posture and the ears are laid flat and back against his head. Submissive body language includes trying to make himself small when he is in your presence. This is an indication that he wants to show he is not a threat. The fur on his body is not standing up and is naturally lying flat against his body. His entire body and facial expressions are relaxed. Happiness is also shown in how he treats you. Licking you is also a sign that he respects you and that he accepts you as his pack leader.

Going first- As has been previously discussed, the leader always goes first. If your puppy respects you, he will not try to get ahead of you. In fact, he will hang back and wait for you to go first. Whenever you are outside, walking up and down the stairs or when someone knocks on the door, your puppy will not attempt to race ahead of you. He will calmly get behind you and wait for your instructions.

Eating first- Alphas always eat first and their food is theirs alone. Your puppy respects you when he does not beg for food or try to steal food from your hand, table or plate. He will calmly wait until you decide to feed him. He will not whine, growl or bark at you while you eat. Whenever you feed your puppy, eat something in front of him (i.e., take a bite from your snack) before giving him his own food. Refrain from giving him something you have just been eating. He will think that your food is also his and will soon be trying to steal it away from you. Alphas never give scraps when they eat.

Place of honor- Alphas always get the best vantage point and the most comfortable space. Prime places for lying or sitting down are all reserved for the alpha. Your puppy respects you if he scoots away when you claim a space on the bed, chair or couch. He lets you get the space you prefer without any hesitation r struggle. He will voluntarily clear any space you desire, even if he has been on it for quite some time before you came. Most dog experts don't see anything wrong about sharing space (i.e., bed or couch) with dogs. Only, make sure not to allow your dog to crowd you out. Also, your dog should get down from the furniture and lie on the floor when you stand up from the couch, bed or chair. This means that your puppy recognizes he is only allowed in your personal space if you give him your permission and only when you are there with him.

Moving out of the way- Your dog shows respect if he moves out of the way. Never step over or walk around your dog. This will make him feel that you are more in his way than he is in yours. When your puppy lies and sits in your way, make him move out.

Allows handling- A puppy who respects his owner will allow himself to be handled. He will not growl when his needs are being attended to. He will be calm when he is groomed and bathed. He is also relaxed while flea control is placed, when his nails are getting trimmed, etc. He will not try to get away even if he dislikes the activity very much.

Breaks eye contact- Eye contact is crucial in establishing leadership. When your puppy respects you as his pack leader, he will be the first to break away when you look him in the eye. If he stares at you for too long, he might be challenging your authority. Never be the first to look away because this is a sign of submission.

Follows commands- A puppy who follows your rules and commands respects your authority. On the other hand, a puppy that ignores you shows defiance and thinks he can do as he pleases.

Respect is very important; it is crucial in maintaining discipline and order in the home. Without respect, you and your puppy will be in a constant struggle for supremacy. He will ignore your commands and do as he pleases. Training him for anything else will be very difficult because he feels he does not have to listen to you. Your puppy will grow up out of control. He might become very aggressive. He will be difficult to handle. Observing basic hygiene will be very difficult because he won't stay still. He may even bite. Most importantly, both of you will be very unhappy.

Chapter 3 – The Ultimate Guide to Puppy Training Using Shaping Technique

There are many methods used to train puppies and adult dogs to behave in certain ways. One training technique to consider is the shaping technique. This technique is more formally known as shaping through successive approximations. The main concept of this training technique is taking a behavior and breaking it down into smaller portions. These portions are reinforced in small increments until the full behavior is achieved.

A good majority of dog trainers hold the shaping technique as the ultimate approach to dog training using the operant conditioning school of thought. Some follow it to the letter while some use the shaping technique as a portion of a multi-part program.

Scientific Background

The shaping technique is based on the idea that a behavior is variable. There are small variations to how a behavior is done each time it is repeated. It may be faster or slower, higher or lower, bigger or smaller, harder or softer, etc. There will always be something different, which may be noticeable or not.

If you want your puppy to be perfectly obedient, determine the components of the desired behavior. For example, you want your puppy to learn the "Sit" command. Determine the components of this behavior. For example, when you give the "Sit" command, your puppy will sit up straight, in the proper heel position all within 3 seconds. Setting these parameters will help in more effective teaching. The lesson will be instilled deeper into your puppy's mind. He will be less distracted, too.

So when you start training your dog for the "Sit" command, concentrate on these components. Say, for example, start with the time component. Set a time frame from which you want your dog to follow the command. Say, 3 seconds from the time you voice "Sit", he will sit down. Now, most owners would be happy with just their puppy sitting, not concerned if it took longer with each time. The risk with this behavior is that you are slowly losing your puppy's attention. You might one day wake up and your puppy is no longer responding to your command. You will then have to start training him all over again. To train him in this component, go through the steps in teaching the "Sit" command. However, be mindful of the time. Get a timer. Give only praise or reward if he responded to the command within 3 seconds. Your puppy won't understand at first why sometimes you give him a reward and sometimes you don't. This is where a clicker would come in handy. Get a timer and use the clicker to mark the 3-second mark. Soon, your dog will notice that when he sat down before he hears the clicker, he gets a treat. If he sat down after the clicker is sounded, he does not get any. He will realize that he only gets the reward if he follows the command fast enough.

Don't stop there. Set the bar higher. Click and provide rewards only when he follows the command within 2 seconds. By this time, you would have already established the time component of the behavior.

Uses

The shaping technique is most often used to teach puppies and adult dogs show-ring behaviors. Dogs in these events respond to their owner's commands with lightning fast speeds. You can also do this for your puppy, even if you do not intend to have him join contents and dog shows. Applications for the shaping technique include the following:

- Help dogs achieve behaviors that are often confusing or physically difficult for them to achieve. For example, teaching Greyhounds to obey the "Sit" command.

- Encourage dogs to carry out behaviors that are confusing or mentally difficult to perform. For example, helping a dog wary of crates to enter his new artificial den.

- Fine-tune behaviors that your puppy has already learned to do. For example, teach your puppy to do the "Sit" command faster, closer and straighter.

- Help your puppy to offer behaviors and try new things. It helps to train him to think creatively to solve problems. One way to do this is by engaging your puppy in shaping games like "101 Things That Can Be Done With a Box".

Shaping Techniques

Shaping behaviors can be done in various ways. One way is the lure-prompt shaping technique. It is a hybrid method of using shaping and other training methods. You show the dog how to carry out a certain behavior by luring him with treats. You can also do this by prompting your puppy with a target or body languages. Then, use shaping technique to reinforce increments in the behavior to obtain the final, desirable behavior. For example, to teach your dog to sit, you lure your puppy to the floor with a treat. Once he gets into the sitting position, you mark the behavior by saying "Sit" and give praise. You keep repeating this process until your puppy associates the command with the behavior and you gradually remove the lure.

While some purists of the shaping technique scoff at the lure-prompt technique, this technique has proven effective in training dogs. This technique helps the dog to learn behaviors in less time than the average. However, this technique is deemed somewhat slow for teaching your puppy about creative thinking and free behavior offering. Offering behavior is a movement or action that the dog makes that indicates he is about to do a learned behavior. For example, your puppy makes a motion to sit without being prompted to.

Another method is the basic shaping technique. With this method, a desired behavior is taught to the puppy without any lures or prompting. Then, reinforce the behavior in small increments based on what the dog offers. Then follow up the behavior with free shaping technique. This technique is performing training exercises, without any specific behavior in mind that you wish to accomplish. The free shaping technique is often confusing and least understood by beginner trainers because there is no specific goal behavior in mind.

Basic Shaping

Basic shaping splits behaviors instead of lumping them. Lumping means reinforcing large portions of the behavior—for example, marking the behavior only when the dog has already sat down. Splitting behavior means marking the slightest step towards the goal behavior—for example, marking the behavior when the tiniest movement (e.g., slightest bend) is observed. Keep marking and moving towards the direction of the goal behavior (e.g. full sitting).

This method is requires close observation and patience. A good behavior to try to teach using the basic shaping technique is the "Go to your place" command. Start by designating your puppy's "place". It may be a blanket, a square of carpet or a dog bed in the corner. Visual markers like these may not be necessary but it helps the dog to make the connections more quickly. It also helps to generalize the goal behavior easier. The visual marker can be easily moved to another spot and the behavior is still performed.

Once the "place" is designated, take a step back and observe your puppy closely. Catch the slightest movement your puppy makes towards the designated place. Mark the tiniest head movement, ear flick, or step. The movements do not necessarily have to be towards the exact spot of the place. Towards the general direction of the place will suffice. Mark these offered behaviors and reinforce them. for example, every time your puppy moves his head towards the place, mark it and give him praise or treat. Keep reinforcing the behavior to help your puppy catch on that this is a desirable action. He will soon make deliberate movements towards the place in order to get more of the attention, praise or treat. When he does this, take a much longer time before marking the behavior. Wait a moment so that the behavior builds. If he gets frustrated, he will try harder to gain your attention or response. The more frustrated he becomes, the bigger the behaviors he will exhibit. However, do not hold out too long. If he feels you are ignoring him, he will think he is not doing what you want him to do. He will stop his offering behavior and you would have missed out on the chance. Keep reinforcing until he is close to the place. Once he is, move forward with him but not a step ahead. This would already be prompting or luring.

Reset when your puppy finally reaches the mat. Get you and your puppy to move back several feet and start from step 1. The goal is to teach your puppy to go to the place and not just be on the place. When your puppy offers to go to the place easily, teach him to lie down on the place (e.g., mat, crate, den etc). This exercise teaches your puppy to rest on this place for a time. Add the verbal cue "Go to your place" when your puppy consistently offers to go and lie down on the "place".

If your puppy does not easily offer this behavior, you may need to take a little more time to shape this behavior. Exercise patience. Split the behavior by looking for the smallest movements that you can reinforce. If he keeps staring at you, do not look at him. Look instead at the "place". If he lies down by your feet and naps, get him back up. Have him stand near the place and observe for any indication he makes towards it. Be more observant of any movements you can reinforce. This way, he will be less inclined to lie down again and sleep.

You determine how and how long to go about your shaping process. Some opt to write out a completely detailed plan for shaping behaviors. Some just go about it with a mental picture and work at it as they move along. Sessions last depending on your preferences. No matter how you go about this and for how long, end each session on a high note. That is, end while your puppy is successful and still enthusiastic. This way, your puppy will be excited the next time you have your sessions.

Lure-Prompt Shaping

This method works effectively with breeds that are known for having difficulty learning some common commands. For example, greyhounds are known for being difficult to teach how to sit. Lots of theories were made in an attempt to explain this notorious difficulty. One widely accepted reason is that the Greyhound's unique body shape makes sitting very uncomfortable. Whatever the reason, it is a fact that there are dogs that are more difficult to be taught certain tricks than other dogs. For example, Greyhounds are lean, muscular, and long bodied dogs yet they are particularly reluctant to sit.

For a puppy that is reluctant or finds it especially difficult to follow the "Sit" command, use a lure. Hold a puppy treat close to the tip of the puppy's nose. Slightly lift up the treat. Observe your puppy. If he follows the treat and also lifts up his nose, mark the behavior and give him the treat. Repeat the process. Each time, lift the treat a little bit higher than before. The point in all this is to teach the puppy to follow the treat wherever you place it. Once he learns this, you will be able to lure to do anything you want.

Observe if your puppy finds it easier to follow the treat. Try moving it over his head, further to the right or left, up and down. When he easily follows, it is time to take things a step further. Move the treat farther back over his head and observe for bending of his hind legs. Once you notice even the slightest bend, mark it. Keep holding the treat farther and mark only when you see him bend his hind legs and nothing else. Repeat the process until he eventually gets into the sitting position.

Some would argue that one can simply gently pushing the puppy over his hocks. Some trainers are even successful with this method. However, some dogs just won't sit. Pushing down reluctant dogs may even cause pain. The lure-prompt shaping technique proves more effective for these types of dogs.

This method is a good way to teach a new behavior quickly. However, it does not teach your puppy the link between the treat, the command, and the behavior.

Even so, this is still the best choice for dogs that are difficult to train. This is also the choice for dogs that do not want physical manipulation. They may tolerate being handled for grooming and care activities but refuse during trainings. Try pushing down on the puppy twice. If the puppy still resists, then opt for this lure-prompt method before something untoward happens.

This technique also works for shut-down dogs. It helps to draw out these kinds of dogs and regain their confidence.

Free Shaping

This method is the choice for encouraging puppies that shut down and do not offer behaviors. The free shaping method brings back confidence to the dog because with this method, everything he does is accepted. There is no definite goal in this training technique. Thus, the puppy cannot do anything wrong.

It requires close observation of the puppy. Any indication of offering behavior is marked and then reinforced. Let the puppy initiate by offering behaviors. For example, if your puppy makes a move towards his crate, mark the behavior and praise him for it. Every time he moves towards his crate, you reinforce it. If he stops this behavior, let him be. Do not lure him or prompt him to repeat the behavior. This is more like a passive way on your part. You allow the puppy to set the behavior he wants to do and only reinforce the desired ones.

Some people have difficulty with this technique because they do not have any goal. They do not know what to look for or what to reinforce. The point in all this is to look out for desirable behaviors and reinforce these.

Shaping Activities

101 Thing To Do With a Box – This game helps to teach your puppy to think creatively and develop some problem solving skills. This shaping game will need only any cardboard box. Old ones will do.

Your dog can play this game on a leash. He can pay off the leash if he won't bolt or get easily distracted during the game.

To play, set a chair and a box (or any object) a few feet apart. Sit in the chair and wait for any offering behavior from your puppy. You look for specific offered behaviors to mark and reinforce. The behaviors should be related to the box (or object). This may be a sniff, a step towards the box, a look in the direction of the object or a push- practically anything as long as it has something to do with the box. There is no specific goal or behavior to teach. Random behaviors are all acceptable.

If you notice your puppy repeating a particular behavior (e.g., keeps sniffing), stop marking/clicking the behavior and wait for the puppy to offer another behavior. Or, if you want, pick out specific goal behaviors and reinforce these. For example, you want your puppy to turn over the box. Wait for him to do this on his own, mark/click it and reinforce it. If you want him to put only his front paws in the box, wait for him to do this on his own. Click once he makes this gesture and then reinforce it.

This game promotes confidence in your puppy. As you click more on his random behaviors, it means he is doing more desirable behaviors. It means he is pleasing you and it gives him a boost on his confidence level. It also encourages him to perform more offering behaviors because he feels what he does is accepted. It also promotes creative thinking.

Body Parts – This shaping game helps your puppy to learn to offer behavior. It helps you to understand just how much the shaping technique is effective in training your puppy to perform detailed movements. Even the tiniest ones can be taught.

To start the body parts shaping game, get a chair and sit on it. Get your dog to sit in front of you. Face each other and closely observe your dog's movements. Observe for a flick of the ear, tongue flicker, lifting of the paw, or head turning. Even the tiniest of a body part movement, mark or click it. This is called capturing the behavior. Continue sitting and waiting for the same movement. Keep clicking every time you see it. The goal of this step is to capture the "inadvertent" behavior and reinforce it so that your puppy will learn to offer this behavior more deliberately the next time. Once he starts offering the chosen behavior, you can start to name it. For example, you chose the flick of his ear. Once he starts offering this, give it a name, like "Flick". This way, you have a verbal cue to use when you incorporate it into another trick or to build it up and shape it into a bigger behavior if you wish.

Basic Principles

Here are basic principles to go by in order to make the shaping technique more enjoyable and more effective:

1. Set criteria and raise these in small portions. The increments should be small enough to be achievable. These should be realistic and matches his current capabilities, but should be large enough to push him to go beyond his limits.

2. When training, concentrate on one aspect at a time. Avoid shaping 2 or more aspects at a time. Your puppy will likely get confused, have difficulty or take longer to learn.

3. While you are shaping a behavior or aspect of a behavior, practice the current response on a variable schedule. That is, make some variations on when or where the behavior is performed. For example, teaching the sit command particularly the time variable. Vary when you train. Do this before you raise the criteria or add aspects into the behavior.

4. Relax the old behavior for a while when launching a new aspect or criterion of a goal behavior. This way, it won't interfere with the new lesson.

5. Be a step ahead. That means, planning each step of the shaping training well ahead. This way, you know the next step to take in case your puppy makes sudden, quick progress. You know what has to be reinforced next to keep the momentum going.

6. Consistency is crucial to training, whatever technique you may be using. This same is true when using the shaping technique. Consistency includes the trainer. Do not change trainers in the middle of the training. There can be lots of trainers for one puppy but there should be only one trainer per shaped behavior.

7. Be consistent but learn to adjust. That is, if your puppy failed to make any progress after a few sessions, find another shaping plan. There are many ways to arrive at the same goal.

8. Consistency means continuity of each session. Do not interrupt the sessions as much as possible. For example, in the middle of a shaping session and your phone rings, do not drop the session to answer. Your puppy will see this as a negative reinforcement. He will think he is doing something wrong but don't know what. It will confuse him and will probably set him back

on the training. When something else requires your attention, taper off and end the session on a high note, even if it seems abrupt. If you can, wait for the behavior and then wrap it up. Or just wrap it up with a clap and say "Good job". Pat your puppy or show affection then leave to attend to other things.

9. Learned behaviors have a tendency to slip away. If you see that your puppy "forgets" or is slowly becoming less enthusiastic about a learned behavior, that means it's time for a review. Go though the shaping process you used in teaching the behavior. This time, use reinforces that are easily learned. This way, the entire shaping process is quickly passed through. This time is meant to be a refresher.

10. Always end each session on a good, successful and happy note. Even if the session was particularly frustrating, always end on a high note. Show that you are still pleased with your puppy's efforts. This is to make sure he will look forward to the next session.

Chapter 4 – The Ultimate Guide to Puppy Training Using Clicker Technique

Another popular and effective method of teaching your puppy is through clicker training. This training method is based on one of the psychological schools of thought on behaviors. It is based on the concept of marking acceptable and desirable behaviors and giving these appropriate rewards in order to reinforce these.

When your puppy exhibits a desirable behavior, it is marked with a clicker. This small, hand-held device is pressed to produce a distinctive, short click. This "click" is precise in marking the behavior. The puppy hears it better and makes it easier to associate the behavior to the click. Puppies are not for long talks and cheers. A simple click is enough to catch their attention and tell them it is a good one. Not only that, this form of acknowledging behavior is safe and always positive. Clicker training is also a humane way of training, especially for puppies. The experience is not traumatic for dogs at such a young age.

Is it effective?

Some doubt the effectiveness of clicker training. Traditionally, training is either through harsh punishments or treats. The clicker technique does not use any. It teaches behaviors through classical and operant conditioning. That is, a desired behavior is reinforced through association with a consequence.

It is a natural response to associate a place, object, event or person to a specific consequence, whether unpleasant or pleasant. The association strengthens as the same consequence is obtained with each encounter. For example, pain is associated with fire. First encounter with this cause and effect situation would form the association. Over time, the association weakens if there are no more succeeding experiences. For example, on day 1, pain was felt when the hand brushed over a fire. An association is formed: fire=pain. For the next 2 weeks, there is no more succeeding encounters. The association formed on day 1 would have waned. If in the next 2 weeks there is at least 1 more encounter (i.e., another incident of brushing against fire), the association is strengthened. The mind would be reminded of the association made on day 1 that fire=pain. This process is an example of classical conditioning. Behaviors and associations are more accidental, rather than intentional. The person did not intentionally pass his hands over the fire to see what the consequences are. That is why the learned association depends on subsequent encounters in order to be retained. Clicker training starts with this kind of learning.

The other school of thought on learned behavior is operant conditioning. Clicker training is mainly based on this psychology. The learned behaviors that started from classical conditioning are reinforced resulting in intentional behaviors. The learned behavior is better retained. Animals trained this way can remember the learned behaviors years after the lesson was first introduced. The learning process is similar to that of classical conditioning. The difference lies in the 3ʳᵈ factor. In classical conditioning, learning is basically a cause-and-effect association. A dog goes to his food bowl and his owner pours food. This is behavior is repeated as the owner is consistently providing the food. If food is taken away, the dog will no longer go to his food bowl. In operant conditioning, the desired behavior is brought out through an effect but the association is made on a 3ʳᵈ factor. For example, when a dog approaches his food bowl, the clicker is clicked followed by food on his bowl. The cause is the going to the food bowl. The effect is the food. The association is made with the click. Over time, the dog learns to associate the click to food. This way, if he hears the click, he will immediately think of food. The food bowl can be removed from the scenario because the click is now associated with food. So anywhere he goes, if he hears the click, he expects food is coming his way.

This type of association is better in the long run because the dog purposefully learned the behavior rather than by accident. The lesson is retained far better and for much longer.

A lot of trainers believe that the clicker method is much better at teaching behaviors compared to the rewards system. The click marks the exact behavior. The dog is able to better distinguish what specific action earned the reward. For example, compare a classic learning method and the clicker method with teaching the "Sit" command. When the dog sits in the classic learning method, a treat is given. The dog learns to follow the command but in variable ways. He may sit immediately after the command is given or wait a few moments before he does. He may sit for more than 5 seconds or he may stand right up. This is because all the dog learns is that as long as he sits, regardless of how fast he obeys or how long he sits, he gets a reward.

With the clicker method, a more precise behavior is taught. When the command "Sit" is given, a click is only given if the dog sits immediately, say, in less than 3 seconds. No click is given if the dog sits after more than 3 seconds when the command is given. This way, the dog learns that the exact desired behavior is to sit and sit fast. Once this behavior is learned, you can take it further. Click only if the dog sits within 3 seconds after the command is given and stays in the sitting position until you give the signal to "Stand". Behaviors learned this way are more precise.

Also, a click helps the dog to precisely associate his behavior to the reward. Some dogs find it more difficult to make associations between their behavior and the reward. The clicker helps them to focus and make a clear association. For this reason, clickers are also referred to as event markers or bridging signals.

A click is an immediate response. It is short and can precisely mark even the tiniest of movement that is crucial to eliciting a desired behavior. A word may take too long. For example, a signal word is meant to mark the flick of the puppy's ear. By the time the word is uttered, another movement would have been made. With a clicker, once the ear is flicked, a click immediately marks it before any more movements can be done and overshadow the desired one.

Also, a click is more effective than a spoken word because it is only associated with behavior training. The sound is only used when it is being associated with a behavior. It is not heard in any other situation. And it only means one thing, a reward is about to follow the click. A voice varies. It is heard most of the time and has several associations. Also, when giving a command, pitch, tone and inflections vary. The emotions behind the voice also vary. The voice on one training session may sound happier than other sessions. Dogs pick this up more precisely because they are very sensitive to sounds. The differences can be a source of confusion. A click is a click and only has one association-good behavior and a treat follows. This clarity makes it easier for behaviors to be learned. It also helps in improving the relationship between you and your puppy. Training sessions become more fun and interesting.

How it works

The basic concept of clicker training is to mark the behavior at the moment it is performed. It is like taking a picture at the moment the desired behavior is done. This snapshot becomes the tool to model the behavior.

Most often, after 2 to 3 clicks, the animal is able to make the association between the behavior, the click and the reward. Dogs naturally want to please their owners and will repeat the behavior they were doing when they heard the click.

There are just 3 basic steps in clicker training:

1. Get or see the behavior acted out.

2. Mark it immediately by clicking.

3. Reinforce the desired behavior until it is learned fully.

This is a very simple example of giving clicker meaning.

- Sit with your puppy for about 30 minutes. Have a bag of his favorite treats with you but keep it out of your puppy's sight.

- Place a treat in your open hand and the clicker in the other. Do not look in the direction of your puppy.

- If your puppy makes a move for the treat, sniffs it, barks at you, mouths or paws, close your hand over the treat. Wait for him to move away from the treat.

- Click only once and offer the treat.

- Get another treat. Close your "treat" hand and do not look at your puppy. If he makes another move for the treat, do not offer it and continue to ignore him.

- Once he is no longer paying attention to the treat, click once and offer it to him.

- Repeat these steps at varying frequencies. That is, click and offer the next treat after 2 minutes, the next one after 5 minutes, etc. this way, your puppy will not come to expect when the treat is coming. He will instead make an association that he has to wait for the click before the treat. He won't rely on the timing of the treat but on the click.

To make the clicker work, trainers have to wait for the clicker association with the behavior to solidify before a verbal cue is used. That is, you have to wait for your puppy to understand what behavior you want him to perform before you actually use the verbal command, such as "Sit" or "Stay". If you put a cue before your puppy understands what you want him to do, the cues will be useless jabber. Remember that your puppy communicates on a different level. Strings of words are meaningless to them. It is only when you have established an association between the learned behavior and the cue will he understand.

To start introducing the cue, click the behavior a few times. If the puppy gets it every time, he is ready for the cue. Give the cue and wait for the behavior. Your puppy will likely stare at you in confusion. Look away and repeat the cue. If the puppy still didn't do anything, end the session. Remember to end on a good note even if your puppy didn't get the cue. Next time, start with the clicker a few times. Then introduce the clue. Your puppy would tentatively repeat the behavior. Click on it immediately. Do not click at behaviors that were performed before the cue was given.

Your puppy will perform the behavior if he understands the cue. His desire to get a reward will be his driving force to keep doing what you want him to do. However, sometimes a puppy won't perform the behavior. This is not an act of defiance or disobedience. These are the likely reasons that your puppy may not be doing the desired behavior:

- He might not have understood the meaning of your cue.

- He might be confused because he understood the meaning of your cue based on the environment when you first taught it. Changing the environment where you give the cue might be interfering, distracting, or confusing him.

- The reward for the behavior may not be enough to keep him interested in the activity.

Adjust the clicker training plan according to these possibilities. Make sure that your puppy has already understood the clicker meaning before you give the verbal cue. Go back to teaching the verbal cue. Then practice it in different settings. Sometimes, a puppy obeys the Sit and Stay command pretty well while in the home. Once outside, he does not listen. There may be too many distractions keeping him from obeying you. Practice obeying commands in different environments so that your puppy will learn to focus on you despite distractions. Also, get to your puppy well. Know what his favorite treats are and use them for reward. Also, you might be giving him as much attention as he desires. Try to be more affectionate and engaging when you reward him.

Positive vs. Negative reinforcements

Clicker training uses only positive reinforcements or rewards. Using punishment is effective in reducing the frequency of undesirable behaviors. However, it also promotes the development of another undesirable behavior. For example, punishing your puppy for getting up on the furniture will curb that behavior. However, the punishment may also cause your puppy to become more aggressive.

The consequences of punishments are less reliable because there are many possible ways your puppy will react to it. The negative reinforcements are interpreted in several different ways. Harsh punishments may turn your puppy aggressive or shy. It may stimulate your puppy to do better or make him lose confidence in himself. Your puppy may interpret it as a signal to stop the behavior. Or, he may feel you are punishing him not because of the behavior but because you no longer love him. The consequences to negative reinforcements are unpredictable and difficult to control.

Negative reinforcements do not clearly mark an event. It is not often clear for the dog why he is being punished. Most often, the punishment is given long after the undesirable behavior is done. It is rarely in direct connection to a particular action. Hence, the puppy does not know what specific action merited the punishment and is thus likely to repeat the undesirable behavior.

Positive reinforcements always mean the same thing-approval and affection. In whatever setting, behavior or circumstance, a reward always has the same meaning and effect. The puppy will feel loved and accepted. He will repeat the behavior because he knows he will get an approval and a reward for it.

Relationships between the trainer/owner and the dog are more rewarding and stronger. Training sessions are more fun and enjoyable because the energy is a positive one. There is a huge difference in the level of enthusiasm and attitude during the training sessions. The puppy is more motivated to earn rewards. It is natural for both humans and animals to work for pleasurable results than to work hard towards avoidance of punishments. Avoiding punishment does stimulate the pleasure centers of the brain and does not provide much motivation and inspiration. Getting pleasurable rewards stimulates the brain even more and promotes inspiration, creativity, and motivation.

Training Basics

After your puppy has established and understood the link between the clicks and treats, he is ready for the main clicker training process. Follow these guidelines for successful training:

Click on the desired behavior only once. Too many clicks would confuse your puppy, especially if one of those clicks would occur with another movement right after the desirable one. For example, you clicked 3 times when your puppy flicked his ear. At some point, he also turned his head on one of those clicks. Your puppy won't be able to differentiate which of the movements merited the clicks. Keep in mind that 1 click=1 behavior and not necessarily 1 action. If your aim is to teach your puppy to sit, then click only when he is fully in the sitting position. Do not click when he bends his hind legs, click when he lowers his body, click when he is sitting and another click once he is in a stable sitting position. That would be too much. Keep things simple. Click when he has achieved the entire behavior.

Click right on the spot. The moment you see him perform the behavior, click on it immediately. Waiting too long would result in weaker association. Once you see him sit down, click on it immediately. Think of clicking as if you are taking a snapshot. You press the shutter once you see the object in position. Waiting too long reduces the possibility of getting the exact shot you wish.

Click then treat. Just as you need to click immediately on the behavior, you should also be prompt in giving the treat or reward. This will strengthen the association and help your puppy to learn and retain the lesson faster.

Teach one behavior at a time. Do not overwhelm your puppy with lots of different commands and clicks. He will be confused and need more sessions to get the command down pat. For example, you want to teach him to stay, sit and raise his paw. All these can be made in one go but teach him each portion in separate session. For example, clicker train him for the stay command. Take a break then teach him the sit command. Have another break before teaching him to raise his paw.

Train for short periods. Puppies have very short attention spans. Keep training sessions short. Limit these to no more than 15 minutes.

End on a high note. It is important to end the session on a high so stop before your puppy is tired and is losing interest. Even on particularly frustrating session, show you are still pleased. Pat him on the head, show affection and say "well done" or "good job". This way, your puppy will be motivated and eager when your next training session comes.

How to get your puppy to behave the way you want

There are 3 main ways that clicker trainers use to start clicker training. These methods help to get your dog to perform the behavior you want.

Catching

The catching method means you have to catch your puppy while he is performing the desired behavior. This is perfect for puppies that already practices offering behaviors. This method requires you to spend more time with your puppy. Patience and keen observation is required. Take your dog to the living room and wait for him to perform a behavior on his own. Determine what behavior you want to catch or just wait around for anything that you might want to train him for. For instance, wait for him to sit down on his own. Watch him closely. Once he sits, you click on it immediately. Give him a treat right after the click. He'll stand up to get the treat and you can start over again. Wait for him to sit down again then repeat the process. This way, you do not force your puppy to do anything. All you need is to be ready to click and treat.

Shaping

The shaping method teaches and reinforces small acts building towards a new, larger behavior. This is most recommended for behaviors that are not natural for dogs. Stay, sit and roll over are common dog behaviors that they naturally do without any training. Behaviors like "go to your place", "fetch" and "Say Hi (raise paw in the air)" are not natural for them. The shaping method is best for these kinds of behaviors. Each small step towards the desired behavior is taught until the puppy learns the new behavior. For example, teaching your puppy to raise his paw. Clicker train him for the sitting position. Then, clicker train him in small increments towards the raising of the paw. When he shifts his body weight, click and treat. Continue this until he associates the click-treat to the weight shifting. Then click when he lifts his paw from the floor. Continue the click-treat until he eventually raises his paw to a height you want him to.

Luring

You use a treat to lure or coax your puppy to get into the desired position. For example, to get your puppy to sit down, you wave a treat in front of him and have him follow it. You raise the treat higher and over his head until he is forced to tip his lower body into a sitting position. Click-treat once he gets into the sitting position. This can be considered as the more active form of the catching technique. You "force" or lure your puppy to be where you want him to be instead of waiting for him to do the behavior on his own. Learning behaviors is also faster with this method compared to the catching and shaping techniques.

Chapter 5 - The Ultimate Guide to Puppy Obedience Training

In this chapter, you will learn:

1. Preparations For The Puppy Obedience Training
2. The Golden Rules Of Puppy Obedience Training
3. Dog Training Theory: The Essentials
4. How To Use Positive And Negative Reinforcements In Your Puppy Obedience Training
5. How To Use Corrections In Your Puppy Obedience Training
6. Fundamental Exercise # 1: Let's Go
7. Fundamental Exercise # 2: Sit
8. Fundamental Exercise # 3: Down
9. Fundamental Exercise # 4: Stand

Preparations for the Puppy Obedience Training

The first thing you have to prepare is the equipment. The essential pieces for training your puppy are outlined in the last chapter. However, the following pieces of equipment, although not essential, will significantly aid and help you in your puppy training activities because of its usefulness because these will serve as a positive reinforcement for your puppy:

1. Tidbits of soft foods such as sausages, doggie treats, or cheese cubes
2. Their favorite toy
3. A small container of the soft tidbits of foods you will be bringing

The second thing you have to do is to have an appointment with your trusted veterinarian. The purpose of your visit to the veterinarian is to make sure that your puppy does not have any health issues and/or problems that may affect the obedience, crate and potty training that you will do. As such, it will be very beneficial if you will deal with any health issue and/or problem at the outset before things get out of hand.

In addition to the health problems and/or issues, you also would want to ask questions about your puppy's breed. Ask about the unique needs, characteristics and behaviors of you puppy. This way, you will be able to adjust your training accordingly to the breed of your puppy.

The third thing you have to do is to learn to hold your leash properly. Make sure to free up the leash when your puppy is doing something correct. This is a form of encouragement so that he would learn to do the right thing and behavior every time.

The Golden Rules of Puppy Obedience Training

Here are the 10 golden rules of puppy obedience training:

1. Keep your puppy on leash during the training proper
2. Do not allow your puppy to get distracted during the training proper
3. Avoid feeding your puppy at least 4 hours before the training sessions
4. Avoid having a training session if your puppy was not able to sleep the night before
5. Avoid having a training session if your puppy had exercised heavily during the morning or a couple of hours before the training session. Your pup might be tired and will not be as responsive to your activity.

6. Be patient with your puppy. Remember, your puppy is like an infant so it will not be able to easily grasp concepts

7. Practice having a training session when your puppy has been sleepy the whole day in order to increase his energy levels

8. Consistent practice is the key to mastery. As such, perform a lot of practices with your puppy for maximum results. For beginners, a training session should be at least 45 minutes.

9. If your puppy disobeys your commands, do not shout or physically hurt him. The problem is with the trainer, not with the puppy.

10. Always observe proper hygiene. It would be very beneficial if your puppy had taken a bath several hours before the training session

Dog Training Theory: The Essentials

The basic training of dogs and puppies are generally divided into three stages. These are:

1. The teaching stage
2. The correction stage
3. The proofing stage

 In the first stage (the teaching stage), what you are doing is to associate a command or a specific word with a desired behavior or action that you want it to have. For example, this is the stage where you will show the puppy how to "Sit."

In the second stage (the correction stage), as soon as you realize that your puppy understands the desired behavior or action that you want him to take, it is now time to correct any misinterpretations in the commands. How do you properly execute this? Simply put, if your puppy correctly performs a desired behavior or action after your command, give him praise, some tap in the head and a food tidbit. This will serve as a positive reinforcement to the puppy you are training.

In the third stage (the proofing stage), as soon as you realize that the puppy can now consistently perform the desired behaviors and actions correctly as a direct response of your commands, it is now time to use some form of distractions. These distractions serve as a tool to enable your puppy to have mastery over the learned commands and subjects that was practiced.

How to Use Positive and Negative Reinforcements in Your Puppy Obedience Training

Positive reinforcements

Positive reinforcements refer to things or actions that your puppy will enjoy. In addition, positive reinforcements also refer to things or actions that will make your puppy happy and motivated to follow the commands that you are training him for. Now, what you can do is to provide your puppy with a positive reinforcement every time your puppy performs a desirable action or behavior. A positive reinforcement must have the following four elements:

1. A genuine and enthusiastic verbal praise
2. A food tidbit of the puppy's favorite treat
3. A time where the puppy can play with his favorite toy
4. Stroke and pet your puppy

Negative reinforcements

Negative reinforcements refer to things or actions that your puppy will interpret as negative. In addition, negative reinforcements also refer to things or

actions that will reduce the likelihood that your puppy will perform an undesirable action or behavior again. Negative reinforcements include pulling the leash such that your puppy is unbalanced and uncomfortable. As long as the puppy discontinues the unwanted action or behavior, you can release the leash or just loosen it a bit in order to bring back the puppy's comfort.

How to Use Corrections in Your Puppy Obedience Training

One of the most essential factors of obedience training is the correction. Remember that as your puppy learns new stuff and commands, he progresses into a dog that can respond to commands quickly. In other words, once your puppy masters your commands, it is as if your puppy has an intuitive feel on how to execute a .given command immediately after commanding him.

When it comes to corrections, take note that it is important to always apply corrections quickly. Another thing to consider is that make your corrections as straightforward as possible. As your puppy corrects his behavior or action, do not forget to provide him with a positive reinforcement. This will embed in your puppy's mind that what he just did is the correct action or behavior within the command that was given.

Fundamental Exercise # 1: Let's Go

The let's go exercise is an exercise designed to warm up your puppy's muscles for a strenuous activity. This means that your puppy will be much easier to control and calmer once you make him or her perform other exercises. In addition, it is also a valuable exercise to provide your puppy with an avenue to burn up some of the energy that has been stored up in his or her body for a long time.

A step by step guide for the let's go exercise:
1. Secure the leash and place the same on your puppy. Hold the leash.
2. Allow your puppy to play with the leash for the time being without any pressure.
3. Afterwards, walk backward until you feel the tension of the leash.
4. Walk forward until you feel the tension of the leash.
5. Walk sideward until you feel the tension of the leash.
6. Once you notice that your puppy turns or looks at you, follow it up with the words, "Good Dog!"
7. After complimenting your puppy, make sure that his or her attention is directed to what you are saying and not to anything else. Avoid any distractions such as toys and other animals such as other house pets.
8. Once his or her attention has been locked, command your puppy with the words, "Let's Go!" and walk towards the park, the garden, or the garage. Make sure that your puppy follows you with the leash until you reach your preferred destination.
9. Repeat the exercise for at least 7 times.

The Let's Go and Recall Exercise

 As a follow up to the let's go exercise, the purpose of the let's go and recall exercise is to simulate real training sessions where you should expect your puppy to come back to you or go to his or her original position.

Hence, the first thing you need to do in this follow up exercise is to make sure that your puppy is a fair distance from you (at least a few meters). In addition, you should also make sure that your puppy is neither looking at you nor in your direction. Now, with a commanding voice, call out your puppy's name together with the word, "Come!"

The first thing that will happen is that your puppy will look at you. At this point, this development is enough. Now, using a high pitched voice, compliment him or her with the excited words of, "Good Dog!" In addition to this, make sure that in an inviting manner, 1) widen and open your arms; and 2) squat your legs to your puppy's level. This action is actually a dog body language tactic that is specifically designed to encourage the puppy to come to you.

Keep complimenting your puppy with the words, "Good Dog!" until he or she reaches you. At this point, pat your puppy in the head. Afterwards, you can perform the first let's go exercises for at least seven times until your puppy fully masters the let's go and recall exercises.

Fundamental Exercise # 2: Sit

The sit exercise is the most effective training exercise to keep your puppy controlled and behaved. As such, the best way to use the sit exercise is whenever your dog performs undesirable acts, is misbehaving, or is becoming out of control by biting, jumping around the house, and constantly barking.

Remember that your goal is to eventually train your puppy to sit whenever you stop walking. This is due to the fact that you want your puppy to be in full control of his or her actions at all times.

Whenever your puppy is in the sit position, he or she has no choice but to pay full attention to you and to what you are about to say. As such, the sit exercise is very useful in gaining control over your dog whenever you stop the other exercises mentioned in this Chapter.

A step by step guide for the sit exercise:
1. Make sure that your puppy is in the sit position by your left leg.
2. Secure the leash of your puppy. Make sure that the leash is properly placed
3. Afterwards, place the leash of your puppy over your hip of the left leg.
4. Take a couple of forward steps then stop and say, "Heel!"
5. Afterwards, command your puppy with the word "Sit!"
6. While commanding your puppy to sit, place both of your hands at the waist of your puppy. Hopefully, placing your hands at your puppy's waist will trigger him or her to sit.
7. However, in the event that your puppy did not sit despite holding his or her waist, this is the proper time to slowly but gently push your puppy into assuming the sitting position.
8. Once your puppy learns to assume the sit position without your interference in step 7, make sure to praise your puppy with the words, "Good dog!" Use a high pitched voice in order to emphasize the compliment. In addition, make sure to physically pet your puppy's head and body.
9. Repeat the first fundamental exercise (Let's go)
10.   Repeat steps 1-9 for at least 7 times.
11.   Once you complete this exercise, you and your puppy are now ready for the next exercise to be done in the next training session.

Fundamental Exercise # 3: Down

Reminder: Make sure to train your puppy one step at a time. This means that it is not sensible to train all the 5 fundamental exercises in a single day or afternoon. In other words, once you and your puppy have completed the first and second fundamental exercises, it will be beneficial to wait for at least a day before moving on to the other exercises.

 The down exercise means that your puppy will be lying on the ground or on the floor. This down position exercise puts you at an authoritative and master position over your dog. This is because the down position exercise has basis on the behavior of animals. According to research on animal behavior, whoever can make another lie down is the master or authority of the one who lies down. As such, this exercise is very important in establishing your authority over your puppy. Whenever you see that you have not sufficiently established your authority over your puppy, you can go back and follow the instructions mentioned in the "Using your voice" part in Chapter 1.

A step by step guide for the down position exercise:
1. Place your puppy in the sitting down position.
2. Stretch and then place the leash at your feet.
3. Step on the leash.
4. Kneel on the leash.
5. Have your right hand at your puppy's shoulders.
6. Have your left hand at your puppy's legs.
7. With a commanding voice, say your puppy's name together with the command, "Down!" while your hands are at the puppy's shoulders and legs. This will provide your puppy with the instinctive idea to lie down on the floor or on the ground.

8. Once your puppy reaches the ground, make sure to give him or her praise and a pat on the head.

9. In order to keep your puppy steady on the down position, command him or her with the words, "Steady!" while resting your hand on his or her shoulders and hips.

10. Once you are sure that your puppy will settle, release your hands.

11. Once released, command your puppy to move to the place where you will perform the next exercise.

12. Some puppies will exert authoritative actions. This is especially true for dominant canine breeds. If this is the case, gently step on the leash as closely to your puppy's head as possible and command him or her with a strong high-pitched "No!"

Fundamental Exercise # 4: Stand

The stand exercise will be a very handy tool for managing your puppy's life. For example, when you go to the dog salon, it will be easier for the service providers to cut nails, bathe, clean the ears, and groom your puppy once you taught him or her the stand position. In addition, it will be easier to bring your puppy to the veterinarian for some medical examinations once your puppy recognizes your command for him or her to stand.

A step by step guide for the stand position exercise:
1. Command your puppy with the sit position.
2. Hold the puppy's leash in your hand.
3. Your left hand or right hand must be at your puppy's collar.
4. Using a high pitched voice, command your puppy by telling him or her to "Stand!"

5. If your puppy does not rise, use the puppy's collar to make him rise by gently pulling it upwards. Once he or she does, praise your puppy with the words, "Good dog!" In addition, pat your puppy in the head.
6. Once your puppy associates the word, "Stand!" with rising up, it is now time to perform the exercise for at least 7 more times.

Chapter 6 – The Ultimate Guide To Puppy Impulse Control Training

In this chapter, you will learn:

1. The Definition Of Impulse Control
2. The Best Time To Do Impulse Control Training
3. The Importance Of Impulse Control Training
4. The General Goal In Puppy Impulse Control Training
5. The Basic Principles In Impulse Control Training Of Your Puppy
6. How To Train Your Puppy To Sit And Stay
7. How To Train Your Puppy To Stop Charging For The Door
8. How To Train Your Puppy To Leave Or Drop It
9. How To Train Your Puppy To Settle

The Definition Of Impulse Control

Puppies are impulsive creatures. That is their nature. To do things without really thinking about any consequence or regard for oneself or others is but a natural thing for a puppy to do. This behavior will not be resolved on its own as the puppy grows older. The solution is something that has to be taught to the puppy. This is where impulse control training comes in.

In a puppy's world, impulse control is similar to a person's ability to remain calm and in control whatever the situation is. It is also equivalent to the ability to delay gratification or to restrain one's immediate desires, temptations, or impulses to do something that might cause harm to other people or to one's self. In short, to learn how to control impulse is to learn how to exercise self-restraint or self-control. Just like a baby, a puppy has no impulse control. However, with early and adequate training from his owner, impulse control can be developed.

A puppy has no idea of how things work in the beginning, too. He has to learn that he cannot have anything he wants anytime he wants it. The urge must be suppressed until the desired object is either available or okay to be possessed. Examples of these would include food, toys, or things owned by other people or other pets.

A puppy must also learn that not all actions are beneficial to him or her. Therefore, the likeliness to perform something must be within the allowed tasks of the owner only. If there is no given approval from the master or owner, the puppy must not perform such tasks. Examples of these are charging through doors, jumping on the owner or other people, nipping, playing, barking loudly, and behaving wildly and playfully even when asked to stop. A puppy would do anything to satisfy the urge unless proper training on how to control his impulses would be done. Otherwise, he would turn out to be an unruly, misbehaved, and disrespectful dog when he grows up.

The Best Time To Do Impulse Control Training

Curbing the impulsivity of the puppy should be a top priority of the owner. The earlier you train, the better it would be for him and for you and for your entire household. Puppies are easier to train than adult dogs. Keep this in mind so that training would not be more difficult for you and your puppy. However, do not think that it is a hopeless situation for you to train your dog if he is already 3 years old. It may take some time and lots of efforts, but it could be done.

Just like a baby left to himself, that baby would grow up to be a spoiled brat if his parents did not train him to be behaved or to control his impulses. By the time he is 2 or 3 years old, it would be difficult to curb his tantrums and impulses. You, as the parent, would have difficulty tightening the reins, so to speak.

Your baby would cry and throw tantrums everywhere and there would be nothing that you can do. You would not want that to happen, right? The solution is simple: Teach the child to be disciplined as early as possible. For the puppy, you would not want him to chew everything he sees or jump on you to have that food or get your attention. Practice impulse control training early on.

The Importance Of Impulse Control Training

A puppy is not born well-mannered. That trait has to be taught to him. When your puppy sees food, his tendency is to run and get that food. If he sees a cat, it is typical for him to have the extreme desire to chase it. That is normal. If he sees you, he would love to jump on you and play with you. These are not unusual behaviors. However, if you let your puppy retain those behaviors and do nothing about them, they could cause you problems later on and they could cause danger, not only to your puppy but to you and other people as well.

There were many dogs that got hurt or died because they were hit by cars when they suddenly ran wildly or enthusiastically outside the gate. If you will not teach your puppy self-control, that could happen to him, too. That could cause damage or death to the driver and passengers of the car as well. This tragedy could be avoided by a simple remedy — teaching your puppy impulse control.

At other times, a puppy that has not learned to stop jumping on people, especially guests, could also cause harm both to himself or the person. If the guest was frightened, he could hurt the dog as a reflexive defense mechanism to protect himself. On the other hand, if the puppy was frightened by the response of the person, he could bite that person to protect himself in turn. In both cases, a simple training on impulse control could prevent this misfortune.

When you train your puppy to be polite and behaved and to act accordingly at all times, you would accomplish two basic things:

> ➢ Appropriate behavior at any given situation, and
> ➢ Protection from any form of danger.

Do you see now how important it is to train your puppy to control his impulses as early as possible?

The General Goal In Puppy Impulse Control Training

Your primary purpose in doing this training is to teach your puppy how to resist or curb his impulses until the acceptable time and commands are given. The puppy should be able to manifest a patient and compliant behavior so that his desired actions would be satisfied only when the owner gives him a go-signal. The puppy would learn how to delay immediate gratification by restraining himself from the desired object unless permitted to do so. The puppy should learn to obey or comply with your commands than do what he wants by himself.

The Basic Principles In Impulse Control Training Of Your Puppy

As you have learned in the previous chapters, a certain action will be repeated and a behavior will be established if the desired outcome is achieved. The reinforcement theory runs on this premise. For instance, if the dog was under the table and you handed him food when he jumped on your knee, the lesson that he learned was to jump on you if he wanted food.

To curb this unwanted behavior or tendency, you must establish the rules to the puppy. Here are the basic principles to remember when you are training your puppy to be patient and compliant even when he is excited about something.

1. *Reinforce learned positive behaviors.* Practice of simple commands which require self-control such as "Sit", "Stay", Leave," and "Down" is a good way to start the impulse control training of more complicated commands. You could motivate your puppy to continue the positive behavior and even add more appropriate behaviors through exciting rewards.
2. *Identify what your puppy wants and why and that would be the reward.* Example, you want to inhibit the impulse of your puppy to run inside or outside through the door or gate. Therefore, the reward here is going through doors. Using that information, your training will center on this with the reward (in this instance, passing through the door) being awarded to the puppy according to the terms of the owner and not the puppy's.
3. *Assess what the puppy does to get the reward* (going through doors). For instance, running ahead of you toward the door and going in or out as soon as you open the door are the actions that your puppy would do as the reward.
4. *Be patient. Now that you are aware of your puppy's actions, start the training.* Pick the behavior to be rewarded. In this case, the puppy should learn to wait for you before he can go out or in or pass through the door. As the puppy is used to you opening the door to let him through, he would appear so excited when you

are near the door already. Do not immediately open the door.

5. *Be consistent*. The change in behavior will not take place after a day's training. In most cases, retraining and recalling may be needed. Be on the lookout for teachable moments and grab those opportunities to strengthen the training you are giving your puppy.

6. *Practice in less exciting environments first*. If your puppy gets super excited when you are approaching the gate, start with the bedroom door first where there is less excitement for him. If the behavior is learned, move to a more exciting environment for him, which could be the front door. Again, when the desired behavior is achieved, go to the most challenging one, which, in this case, is the front gate.

7. *Place consequences for impulsive behaviors*. This is to discourage the repetition of such behaviors. Examples are withholding the reward for breaking the command or using special words, such as "wrong" or "oops" to indicate wrong actions or behaviors.

8. *Make the training sessions short and fun*. Focus on what your puppy is doing right than what he is doing wrong. If he enjoys the training, he is more likely to learn and be excited for the next training session.

Here are some important tendencies that need to be controlled to secure the safety of your pet and yourself, too, as well as that of other people and pets. Using the basic principles stated above, curb your puppy's natural desires for the following: charging through doors, eating or getting things from the floor or ground, being overly excited, and being restless and active when the situation calls for stillness or calm. Here is the first skill to be learned.

How To Train Your Puppy To Sit And Stay

This exercise will benefit you more than the dog, actually. With this one, you are training the puppy to remain seated and steady unless you ask him to move. There are many uses for this trick. First, when leashing the puppy, this command will keep him steady while you complete the task. Also, you can keep the puppy from jumping up and down toward you or other people, or going through the door or up the stairs.

1. Stay on the right side of the puppy and sit beside him. Both of you should face the same direction.
2. Attach the leash.
3. Hold the leash close to the dog's collar. Apply tension. It should not be too tight to cause discomfort to the puppy.
4. Give the cue "Stay." Step in front of your puppy and face him. Maintain the tension in the collar.
5. Wait for at least 10 seconds and then go back to his side. Release the tension of the collar and praise the puppy or give him a treat.
6. Repeat the exercise. This time, step a bit farther away from your puppy and time it a little longer. Do this several times in a day until your puppy has mastery of the exercise.
7. Try to add some distractions while doing the exercise. Do this until your puppy becomes comfortable doing the Sit and Stay cue even without the leash on. You could practice this every time your puppy comes to greet you.

How To Train Your Puppy To Stop Charging For The Door

Puppies love to charge for the door for a variety of reasons. Maybe they saw a cat enter that door. Maybe you have just arrived and they want to play with you inside. Or maybe it's the opposite — the puppy has been confined inside the house for several hours and now he wants to go out and play outside. Whatever the reason is, learning how to curb that impulse to run wildly inside or outside could be safer for you and your puppy.

Other Reasons Your Puppy Charges Toward Doors

1. To find a mate. If your dog is by himself, having a partner is a primary goal for him. Since he is already aware that there is no other puppy except himself inside the house, he knows that he would find his mate outside; hence the wild run toward outside as soon as an opportunity comes.
2. Fear. A door is usually the first cause for a puppy experiencing pain. Most of the time, the door has closed in on him or he has been pinned by it. Whatever the reason, the puppy does not want to be anywhere near the door and so he rushes past it, either going inside or out.
3. Competition with other dogs. If the puppy has other puppies or dogs with him, passing through a door is like competing in the Olympics — whoever comes in or out first is the winner. And so, there is this wild rush to the door each time.

Teaching Your Puppy To Sit And Stay At Doors

Whatever the reason for your puppy's tendency to charge at doors, you must teach him how to sit and stay at the door. He must also learn how to wait for your instruction before he can move through a door. This is simply done by reinforcing the Sit and Stay tricks.

Put a leash and then approach the door. While holding the leash, make sure that it is loose enough so as not to hurt the puppy. Ask your dog to sit and then stay. Open the door slowly, just about an inch wide. Again, reinforce the sit and stay commands. If your puppy stands up immediately to go through the door, close the door quickly.

Ask the puppy to sit and stay again. Repeat this exercise until the puppy sits and stays for at least 3 seconds even when the door is open. Give your dog a tasty treat after this small victory. This is to reinforce the desired behavior of compliance. Pause for another three seconds. This time, release the puppy from the leash. Make a signal to the puppy that the training session is over by saying a special word like "okay." Then, you can completely close the door or if you need to go outside with the puppy, walk through that door with your puppy.

Practice the above exercise for longer periods of time. Open the door gradually and the puppy should remain in the sitting and staying position for longer periods of time. Also, make the opening of the door wider than 1 inch. The puppy's behavior should be the same. He needs to wait for your signal before he can pass through the door. Do not forget the treats whenever your puppy does something right. Use your special word so that your dog knows that it is time for him to get up from the sitting position and pass through the door.

Other Considerations

Your actions would vary a little according to the reasons. If the reason for curbing his impulse to charging for the door is that your puppy is looking for a mate, spaying or neutering them may be part of the solution (plus it could solve the problem of overpopulation of dogs). Then, proceed with the discussed exercise above.

If your puppy charges at doors because of fear, the initial action that you must do is to discover what is the cause of his fear. Find out what the puppy is afraid of. Then try to eliminate the cause of fear. If that is not possible, you must teach the dog to be unafraid of that thing through desensitization and counterconditioning process. Only then can you proceed with the discussed exercise above.

What Is The Desensitization Process?

This is a technique to conquer fear or phobia over a thing or a person. This strategy involves exposing the puppy to what he is afraid of and trying to eliminate the fear, slowly but surely. For instance, if the cause of fear is the sound of the door squeaking each time it opens, get the puppy near the door and let him hear the squeak for a short time. Be at your puppy's side and provide support. Try to speak soothing words to him to lessen his fear. Hold him closely to you, too.

The next time you do this, it should be for a longer period of time and you should be less close to him as well. This is to be repeated until he has totally overcome the fear of the sound of the door. Then you can do the rest of the activity as discussed until he has mastered control over the impulse to run through doors.

What Is Counterconditioning?

This is another technique in trying to remove the fear or phobia of your puppy of something. Counterconditioning is simply "re-teaching" your puppy, making the feared object a source of pleasure or fun for him instead. Let's go back to the squeaky door example. If that is the fear, find a toy that has a similar sound. When the puppy gets used to playing with the toy with that similar sound, the fear of the squeaky sound will be eliminated. Instead, every time the puppy hears the sound, he associates that with fun or play.

How To Train Your Puppy To Leave It Or Drop It

Control over the impulse of trying to eat or get something that was dropped could have infinite benefits, too. For instance, when a medicine pill or drug is dropped, it could cause some hazardous side effects to the puppy if he ingests it. Or, while walking in the park, your puppy found a half-eaten hamburger on the grass. This command might save, if not his very life, then at least his stomach. However, what if it is chocolate? It is a known fact that chocolates can be deadly to puppies. This training then could mean the very life of your puppy.

How To Do The "Leave It" Impulse Control Training – Part 1

Discover a high value but "forbidden object" for your puppy. A good example is a freeze-dried liver cube. Allow him to sniff, nibble ,and lick it but do not let your puppy have it.

Holding the cube, say, "Leave it," and then immediately put it on the floor just under your foot (Note: be sure that you are wearing a pair of rubber shoes). Your puppy's instinct is to sniff and get the treat under your foot. Do not allow him to have a taste of the cube or else that would be a form of reinforcement for him.

Just let the puppy be. Do not repeat the cue "Leave it." When the puppy finally stops trying to get the treat (it may take some time but he will), the split second that he stops trying or he looks away, click your clicker to "mark" the moment. Or you could praise him or say "good dog" and then give him a treat.

When he tries to search for the treat again, just wait. It is vital that you do not give him the cue of "leave it" this time. Again, when he stops or looks away, click and then praise him and give him a treat. This is done to reinforce the behavior of looking away from the "forbidden object." Repeat this several times.

After several successful repetitions, get the cube from the floor, show it to your puppy, give him the cue "leave it" and again, place the cube under your foot. The next step is a more challenging one. Lift up your foot so that the cube would be exposed. Keep your foot near it in case there is a need to cover the cube (this will occur after the first several minutes of exposure). Be very alert for clicks and treats every time the puppy looks away from the treat. If he tries to get the cube, just cover it with your foot. Reward him every time he looks away from it.

How To Do The "Leave It" Impulse Control Training – Part 2

When you can place the cube on the floor and the puppy is not attempting to get it, do this next step, which is called "Leave it/drop it." Show the cube to the puppy. Say the cue: "Leave it." Then, make a well-placed drop. If you drop it in the wrong place, for instance, near the jaw of the puppy, he would be able to get it and the training is ruined. Instead, drop it where you can do a "body block" in case he attempts to get the cube. Do not say "leave it." Just try to protect or cover the cube so that the puppy won't get near it. When he looks away, click and give him a treat.

Next, get the cube and say "leave it" while you drop the cube. Repeat this several times until you get to the point that you do not have to protect or cover the cube because the puppy is not trying to get it anymore, even when you drop it near him. Do not forget the click and the treat for each time the puppy ignores the forbidden object.

How To Do The "Leave It" Impulse Control Training – Part 3

This is just the reverse of part 2. This time, drop the cube and then say the cue "leave it." Why is this important? There would be times that you would not be able to give the cue before the drop, in real life. Most of the time, there is the drop first and then you'd try to stop your puppy from eating it.

Here is how to do it: Position yourself again in such a way that you would be able to cover the cube if needed. Drop the cube and then give the cue "leave it" (make your voice cheerful now). Do this several times. When the puppy has finally mastered the art of the "leave it" cue, then make it more interesting by bringing your puppy to an alley (inside your house first) where there are many objects on the floor. When you reach the first object, give the cue. When he obeys, give the click and the treat. Go to the next object and repeat the process until you reach the last object.

By this time, your puppy is ready for the real thing. You could bring him to the park or anywhere else and there will be no fear of him eating or getting things or items on the ground.

How To Train Your Puppy To Settle

Another important impulse to control is your puppy's natural fondness of action and movement. You see them jump, fetch, run, and even go in circles just to catch their tails. There is so much energy and enthusiasm. However, this could be tiresome — not only to the puppies but to the owners as well. It's time to curb this behavior. The puppy must learn the cue "Settle." As with almost all trainings, one should start very early in a puppy's life to be able to establish the behavior easily.

The main objective of this exercise is not to deprive the puppy of enjoyment. This is to train him how to be calm when he is overly excited. Why is this important? This will save the puppy and his owner unnecessary "accidents" due to the puppy's extreme excitement. When a puppy follows the order of "settle," it could spare the owner time and effort in running after his puppy that is in turn, might be chasing after a cat or a rodent, too.

Step-By-Step Techniques For A Puppy To Learn How To Settle

Check out the techniques below:

1. Put your puppy on a leash. Have him settle down beside you for 5, 10, or 30 minutes. When you give the cue to "settle" or "settle down," the puppy should learn how to be calm and quiet in a spot. He could do this either in a lying or sitting position.
2. Allow the puppy to stretch out, curl up, lie on its back, or assume the down position (sphinx-like). However, standing up and playing with you or with a toy is not allowed.
3. You can coordinate with other members of the family and take turns on doing the "quiet moments." For instance, while the children are studying or when the father is reading his newspaper in the morning, the puppy can also be asked to do the "settle" training. Consistency is key. In no time, you would see that the puppy has developed patience and would remain seated or in a lying position when asked to settle.

4. When the puppy tries to get up or becomes restless, you can put him on a tie-down until he masters the art of being calm and composed.
5. Then, practice a more complicated exercise by going a little farther from the puppy. The puppy should remain as instructed even though you are a bit far from him. Do repetitions of this exercise until the puppy is very compliant to the command.
6. At this point, do not expect that the puppy will behave the same way when he is outside. The "settle" behavior is expectedly more difficult to manage when outside since there are more stimuli that can excite the puppy. Try to do it slowly. Start within your backyard.
7. Incorporate this exercise with walking. How? After a block or two of walking, you sit down and try to read a book or just sit still by yourself. The puppy should also be in a relaxed position. This activity teaches the puppy to control his feelings of excitement. Take a walk again after 10 to 15 minutes and do the same procedure after another block.
8. Incorporate this exercise even during playtime. After several minutes of playing, settle down yourself plus give the cue "settle" to your puppy. Repeat this until there is mastery of this activity.

Here are other things you can do to establish the "settle" impulse control training:

➢ Ignore the puppy's behavior of hyperactivity. Sometimes, the puppy's way of getting your attention is to be overly excited and active. Try not to touch him or play with or even make eye contact with him. The puppy will soon realize that it is not the proper way to get you to notice him.
➢ Keep him busy with other things. Lack of activities can lead a puppy to boredom. When that occurs,

hyperactivity is the result as an attempt to entertain himself. Curb this unruly behavior when you give him "work." For instance, add a little weight to him by letting him carry a backpack (with extra weight on it). Instead of running after cats or squirrels, the puppy will be focused on his "work."

➢ A good way to burn those extra energies that is causing the hyperactivity in your puppy is to take him out for a vigorous walk.

➢ Assess yourself, too. Puppies usually imitate their owners. If you are always on the go, the chance of your puppy being the same is very high. When the puppy sees you as calm and composed, he would actually be the same.

➢ See if aromatherapy could do the trick. Remember that a puppy's sense of smell is very strong. According to studies, just as a human being can experience a relaxed state with different aromas, dogs could, too. Ask your veterinarian which aroma is suitable for your puppy.

Application For Other Impulses

Using the above example, you can also remove other impulsive behaviors of your puppy. Do not do two behavior modifications in one training. As soon as there is mastery of one behavior, you can proceed to the next one, provided that you do retraining and recalling of the first behavior once in a while so that your puppy will not forget the learned behavior quite easily.

Chapter 7 - The Ultimate Guide to Puppy Crate Training

In this chapter, you will learn:

1. The Benefits Of Crate Training Your Puppy
2. Crate Training Your Puppy
3. The Proper Schedule For Crate Training Your Puppy
4. The Proper Duration For Crate Training Your Puppy
5. Timeout
6. Training Home Alone

The Benefits of Crate Training Your Puppy

Often, owners of puppies and dogs are not sure as to whether crate train their pets or not. It is important to take into consideration that crate training has many benefits that you will enjoy as the owner of a puppy. This is opposed to simply confining your puppy to any area around the household. These benefits include but are not limited to the following:

1. Training in the household
   a. By crate training, your puppy will hold his bladder and bowel movements when not in the crate. As such, it will be easier for you because you will not have to worry about your puppy peeing or pooping around the house. In other words, crate training is very beneficial for you and the members of your family or household because a crate trained puppy will not defecate or urinate just anywhere in the house.
   b. In fact, there are puppies that have been trained to defecate or urinate in the bathroom or even in a

separate crate. The other crate therefore, will be used as bed where the puppy sleeps.

2. Avoid chewing things around the house
   a. By crate training, your puppy will avoid chewing things around the house such as slippers, pieces of furniture and even remote controls. Remember that puppies have the natural disposition to like to bite and chew things around. As such, by crate training your puppy, you will not be worried that your puppy will be chewing something without your supervision.

3. Settling down
   a. By crate training, your puppy will learn how to settle down in a single place. Remember that puppies have the natural disposition to run around the house. By placing your puppy in the crate (in a single place), you teach him to stay put in one location at a time.

4. Preparation for confinement
   a. By crate training, your puppy will learn how to be confined in a single place and a single location. This is an important skill especially when you have the intention to travel with your puppy in the near future. As such, when travelling, you can now place your puppy in the crate without worrying about the stress that your puppy will incur. The reason is that since your puppy has been trained in the crate, your puppy is already used to being confined to it.

Crate Training Your Puppy

The proper way to crate training your puppy is through slow progression. You would not want to throw your puppy into the crate and expect that

everything will be fine. The first thing you can do to make your puppy adjust to his or her new surroundings is by making the crate as comfortable as possible by putting blanket or some small pad. The second thing you can do in order to make your puppy feel comfortable is by feeding him inside the crate. Always remember to leave the crate door open so that your puppy would not feel isolated or imprisoned. If you have a toy that is safe and non-toxic, you can bring the toy together in the crate so that your puppy will be able to play and chew it.

The Proper Schedule for Crate Training Your Puppy

In order to build a proper schedule for crate training your puppy, you must take into consideration the usual schedule of defecation and urine of your puppy. Most of the time must be spent inside the crate except in times of elimination (defecation or urine). You must build a schedule around this time. For small and young puppies, the usual schedules of elimination (defecation or urine) are as follows:

1. Schedule your puppy to be released from the crate first thing in the morning before drinking water or even before any form of food enters his or her mouth (breakfast)
2. After eating every meal (breakfast, lunch, dinner etc.), release your puppy from the crate for at least 20 minutes
3. After waking up from a nap in the afternoon (for small puppies usually 20 to 45 mins long), release your puppy from the crate for at least 5 minutes
4. For puppies that are not more than 10 weeks old, it would be practical to release them from the crate after every hour or so. The reason for this is that young and newborn puppies have small bladders. This results to frequent elimination of their internal organs.

5. Lastly, schedule your puppy to be released from the crate just before bed time or several hours before a long trip.

The Proper Duration for Crate Training Your Puppy

As a rule of thumb, avoid leaving a puppy in the crate for a very long period. The reason for this is that leaving him in a single place for several hours at a time will force him do his toilet business in the crate – which you clearly do not want to happen. As such, you can train your puppy to keep the crate from being soiled by removing or releasing him or her in the crate every several hours. The following rules are suggested when it comes to putting your puppy in a crate for hours at a time:

1. For puppies that are between 8 and 10 weeks old. The maximum number of hours within which you can put your puppy inside the crate is 1 hour.
2. For puppies that are between 11 and 12 weeks old. The maximum number of hours within which you can put your puppy inside the crate is 2 hours.
3. For puppies that are between 13 and 16 weeks old. The maximum number of hours within which you can put your puppy inside the crate is 3 hours.
4. For puppies that are between 17 and 20 weeks old. The maximum number of hours within which you can put your puppy inside the crate is 4 hours.
5. For puppies that are between 21 and 24 weeks old. The maximum number of hours within which you can put your puppy inside the crate is 5 hours.
6. For puppies that are between 25 and 27 weeks old. The maximum number of hours within which you can put your puppy inside the crate is 6 hours.

 For puppies and/or dogs that are beyond the 27 week mark, you can let

them in the crate for a maximum of 7 to 8 hours depending upon the circumstances. As an additional tip, if you will buy a crate, make sure that it will be large enough to hold when your puppy becomes a full pledged adult dog. As such, you have to study the breed of your puppy in considering the purchase of the crate.

Timeout

There are a lot of times when your puppy will behave badly or become unruly during the crate training process. This unruly behavior includes the following:

a. Jumping up and down in the crate
b. Barking, whining and crying very loudly
c. Nipping at your hands and ankles
d. Biting you

If this is the case, you can implement the timeout strategy in order to keep your puppy behaved and controlled throughout the process of crate training. To put it simply, the timeout strategy is synonymous with the timeouts done usually in professional sports such as basketball and football. In these kinds of sports, whenever a player or a group of players on the court are not executing the game plan as they should (i.e. exhibiting bad behavior), the coach will call a timeout and will usually bench the erring player (unless, of course, the referee is the first to order the erring player to leave the field or court). This means that the player will be ejected.

The same principle is used in the timeout strategy in puppy crate training. In effect, you will remove your puppy from an activity that he or she likes (such as playing with his or her toys  inside the crate) because of unruly behavior. In other words, you will "penalize" your puppy.

Puppy Training Guide 4th Edition

Listed below is a step by step guide in order to implement the timeout strategy in puppy crate training:

1. Set up the situation
   - This means that you will set up your dog for the timeout crate training session.
   - For example, if you do not want your puppy to continue the behavior of jumping up and down the crate while you are eating, a good way to set up the situation is this:
     - ✓ In the dining room, try to act as if you are about to eat your dinner. Make sure that your puppy is watching your actions from inside the crate so that he or she will buy that you are indeed eating.

2. Describe your goal
   - What is the specific goal of your timeout strategy? Make a mental picture of the situation at hand. In this way, it will be easier for you to achieve your goal of suppressing and curbing unwanted puppy behavior while in the crate.
   - This list might be a good starting ground for your specific goals regarding the timeout strategy:
     - ✓ Prevent your puppy from jumping up and down the crate while you are eating dinner.
     - ✓ Prevent your puppy from crying, barking and whining while you are eating dinner.
     - ✓ Prevent your puppy from begging while you are eating dinner.

3. Out
   - Have a word that you will use in order to indicate to your puppy that he or she is about to be isolated. Remember to not simply use the word "No!" The reason for this is that the word "No!" does not really accomplish anything. In fact, the

word "No!" is not the punishment. Instead, the punishment is the isolation in the crate.

- For many people, the usual words they use in order to indicate to the dog that they are about to be isolated are the following:
    - ✓ Buh-bye!
    - ✓ Too bad!
    - ✓ Sorry!
    - ✓ Timeout!
- When used together, it was observed that these words helped the owners of the puppies relax in the event that their puppies should be isolated.

4. Duration of the timeout crate training strategy
- In order to make timeout crate training effective, you must consistently do it with your puppy with a duration of one to two minutes.
- In order to do this consistently, schedule this training session three times a week.
- After two weeks, you will be amazed by the improvement in your puppy's behavior.

Training Home Alone

 Take note that being alone is not something that is natural for dogs, much less for puppies. However, there are a lot of times that you really need to leave the house to deal with certain urgencies and emergencies at work, in the family, or in your neighborhood. As such, it would be beneficial to perform training home alone techniques inside the crate before anything happens.

This simply means that you will train your puppy to be alone inside the crate *while* you are at home. In order to execute this technique, you simply need to provide your puppy with a stuffed Kong while you are doing something else – watching

TV, talking on the phone, eating lunch, brushing your teeth, resting, etc. The purpose of this is to keep him distracted by the stuffed Kong instead of being distracted by your non-presence. In addition, having your puppy inside the crate for short periods of time will enable your dog to experience your non-presence. As such, by the time you will leave for a longer time, your puppy will get used to your absence.

What you should never do is to allow your puppy to run around the house. If you allow this to happen, remember that your puppy will do what his nature tells him or her to do. This means that he or she will pee and/or poop *everywhere* (even in your bed!). In addition, he or she will destroy things around the house and even ingest small items that are not meant to be eaten. Therefore, it is best to place your puppy in the crate, especially if he or she has not yet mastered control of his or her actions.

Chapter 8 - The Ultimate Guide to Puppy Potty Training

In this chapter, you will learn:

1. The Fundamentals Of Potty Training Your Puppy
2. The Proper Use Of Crates As Potty Training Tool
3. Values You Must Have In Order To Be Successful In Potty Training Your Puppy
4. Times When You Should Check If Your Puppy Will Defecate Or Release Urine

The Fundamentals of Potty Training Your Puppy

Potty training, also known as toilet training, is one of the most problematic issues that puppy owners are facing each and every day. This is why the most efficient, effective and stress-free ways on potty training your puppy will be outlined. The fundamental principles and concepts of potty training your puppy are the following:

- Puppies, especially those that are below 15 weeks old, have small bladders. As such, their bodies are not yet well developed. The implication of this fact is puppies cannot go for long periods without defecating or releasing urine.
- Puppies and dogs alike are creatures that are directed by the habits that they previously formed. The implication of this fact is that as the habit forms, puppies will perform defecation and releasing of urine in the same place that they did in the past over and over again.
- As a rule of thumb, avoid potty training your puppies and dogs using papers (i.e., newspapers, and other lengthy papers). The reason is that it teaches your

puppy that it would be perfectly fine to defecate or release urine in the house as long as it is within the paper. The truth of the matter of course is that soiled papers are more difficult to clean as compared to a soiled floor. Also, if you toilet or potty train your puppy using papers, she might form a habit out if it. As such, your puppy will look for papers where he can defecate or release urine. When your puppy becomes a dog, this behavior may no longer be changed or replaced.

- Avoid punishing your puppy in case of poop and urine accidents. This will not be very effective because it only teaches the puppy to fear you. As such, the lesson that he or she should not go to the wrong place is not embedded in the command. All the puppy hears about is the infuriated command and the punishment that you instilled on him. Another result of punishing your puppy for poop and urine accidents is that your puppy will simply try to avoid you at all cost, and will normally perform defecation and releasing of urine anywhere in the house when you are not present. You would not want that to happen, right? Thus, avoid setting up punishments for toilet accidents.

The Proper Use of Crates as Potty Training Tool

 As mentioned in the preceding chapter, crate training will be a very valuable recourse in potty training your puppy. In fact, since puppies are animals that 'den' animals, they can easily adapt and adjust to devote a space as a resting and sleeping place (crate) and devote another place as one for defecation and releasing urine. What you can do is to always put the crate where your puppy is supposed to rest and sleep in a place where there is a person or group of persons regularly. Make sure that this is a place where most of the family members spend a lot of time with. These places include the kitchen, the bedroom, the dining room and the living room.

Values You Must Have In Order To Be Successful In Potty Training Your Puppy

In order to successfully potty train your puppy, you must exhibit the following values:

1. Consistency
   * You need to be consistent in training your puppy for toilet or potty training. Remember that puppies and dogs are essentially creatures of habit. Once you have successfully created a habit for them, they will perform desirable actions such as defecating and releasing urine only in the proper places.
2. Patience
   * Puppies are essentially infant dogs. As such, it is highly improbable that they will be able to master or learn any command that you will tell them, especially when it comes to potty and toilet concerns. Therefore, you have to exercise a lot of patience in potty or toilet training your puppy dog.
3. The use of positive and negative reinforcements
   * As discussed in the previous chapter, reinforcements are a handy way to inculcate actions and behavior that are desirable and to avoid actions and behavior that are unwanted or not desirable.

Times When You Should Check If Your Puppy Will Defecate or Release Urine

When potty training your puppy dog, make sure that you take him or her out to the place where he or she is supposed to defecate or release urine during the following times:

Puppy Training Guide 4th Edition

You must realize that these guidelines for training are not only to direct your puppy in the path he or she must go to grow up into a well-mannered dog, but also for your own good as your pet puppy's master, especially when you are out taking your pet to places and introducing him or her to others. Sometimes it is not the puppy's fault that he is/she is what he is/she is, but the master's. In the same way, when a puppy or any pet's behavior is worthy of praise, then so is his or her master.

Now in this chapter, you will know that one of the best avenues of playing with your puppy is to teach him or her some tricks that both you and your puppy may fancy. This chapter is the ultimate guide to teaching tricks to your puppy and aims to discuss the following points with utmost relevance and accuracy:

1. Establishing a Playful and Friendly Relationship with Your Puppy
2. Preparations for Teaching Tricks
3. Basic Tricks You Can Teach To Your Puppy

These guidelines will aid you not just in teaching your puppy some tricks for your own and other people's entertainment, but it can also help you improve your relationship with your pet puppy, therefore strengthening your bonds as you advance along the way. The significant role of these guidelines is not so much in simply acquiring a new talent for your puppy; the importance of knowing what this chapter will be teaching is in finding new ways to spend quality time with your pet.

Establishing a Playful and Friendly Relationship with Your Puppy

Just like any other kind of relationship, the one you have with your puppy is important and must be established well while your pet is still young. At the beginning of your relationship with your puppy, he or she must already feel comfortable and safe, above all. This is relevant to the topic of teaching them tricks because once a puppy is already at ease with you, it will become easier for him or her to play with you and to be polite and well-behaved under your command. Here are some ways to establish a good relationship with your puppy.

- Know your puppy.

    Like people, puppies are different from one another. One breed may have a specific need over the other. Knowing your puppy is important if you wish to cater to his or her needs properly, without having to unknowingly sacrifice his or her health and well-being. You may do so by visiting a veterinarian or by researching on the breed of your puppy. Learn about your puppy's body language, and the other ways by which he or she communicate with you. Pay attention to what your puppy likes and what displeases him or her, as well as your puppy's behavior toward different situations. This will also better equip you for when you start to train your puppy.

- Spend time with your puppy.
    Puppies don't like being ignored by their masters. Just like an infant, your puppy also needs some attention. If you

are too busy after a long day at work, you may spend time with your puppy that won't exactly exhaust you further. Try letting your puppy into the living room and rub his head gently while you relax on the sofa, watching TV. This will make your puppy feel that you care enough to spend even just a little time with him or her.

- Properly communicate with your puppy.

    As discussed in the first chapter of this book, there are guides on which tone of voice to use when talking to your pet puppy for different situations, such as the praising tone voice when you want to commend your puppy for doing something good, commanding voice tone for when you need him or her to do something like fetch a ball or establishing authority over the puppy, and the corrective voice tone which is used to let your puppy know that he or she is doing something that should not be done. You may refer to Chapter 1 for a thorough explanation on this, but the main point is you have to communicate clearly with your puppy. In such cases, consistency is the key.

- Control your temper.

    When you are not in the mood to attend to your pet puppy, it is better to dismiss him or her gently rather than end up yelling at your pet because puppies can be really sensitive. If you arrive home tired from work and you are not pleased with what your puppy has done while you were gone (perhaps something like having ripped the drapes to shreds), you can use a corrective tone of voice to let your puppy know that you did not like his or her behavior, but a corrective tone does not necessarily mean shouting at your puppy. Your pet will feel your frustration toward the situation and toward him or her and will feel unwanted. Like any human relationship, controlling your temper in times when you are not in the mood to pacify your puppy can save your relationship from an ugly confrontation.

- Love your pet.

Lastly, just love your pet and show him or her your affection. Without a doubt, this will establish a good relationship between you and your puppy. Puppies can feel when they are loved and when they are not. Have fun with them; treat them like how you would treat any human friend. They are, after all, man's best friends.

Preparations for Teaching Tricks

In any training, preparations must be done to equip one's self with the materials and the knowledge on how you can use it to your advantage. This does not exclude teaching your puppies some tricks. As mentioned numerously throughout this book, your puppy is like an infant. Taking this into consideration, you must be patient with your puppy and must not expect him or her to learn what you teach him or her immediately.

In preparation for this, you will need:

- Props (for tricks that may include items to be played with or retrieved)
- A treat (for when your puppy does it right)

As part of your preparations, warm your puppy up by casually teaching him or her some of the most basic tricks there is. The casualty of the situation would make your puppy feel that you are simply playing. Your puppy will be enjoying the activity without being too pressured to perfect the command. Teaching your puppy to get something is a good start; limit the training to some items that your pet would not grow easily tired of retrieving, like a small ball. You can simply say, "Fetch, boy/girl" and demonstrate to him or her how to get the ball and give it back to you.

Remember that your puppy needs to know if he or she is doing a good job or is doing the wrong thing. You may confirm that he or she is doing the right thing by giving your puppy bits of food. Puppies would know that you are pleased with their actions because they are being rewarded. If the case, however, is the opposite, refuse to give your puppy a food treat. Remember that puppies recognize consistency. You have to be firm with them so that they would know which is bad; as a result, they will avoid committing their mistakes again.

It is quite undeniable that handling a puppy is like handling a person as well. Do not scold your puppy harshly. Sometimes it is not the puppy's fault that he or she finds it difficult to learn the tricks; it might be the trainer's fault. And in the same way that a mother prepares her child for the first day of school, you as a master should also be caring and supportive about your puppy learning new things. Be prepared for disappointments and frustrations because your puppy may not catch up quickly enough on his or her lessons at the pace that you would want him or her to be in—but you should also be prepared for the joys that a puppy can bring once he or she learns successfully. Your puppy's triumph is yours as well.

Basic Tricks You Can Teach To Your Puppy

Teaching tricks to your puppy is a really enjoyable activity. Once your puppy has started undergoing his or her puppy training and is already manifesting signs that he or she would like to learn, teaching him or her a few tricks would be easier. But compared to your puppy's training, teaching him or her a couple of puppy tricks could mean play time. In this case, masters should avoid teaching their puppies tricks in between or during their puppies' training so that they may not confuse the time when they need to be serious about the task at hand and when they can fool around with their masters.

In this sub-chapter you will learn a few basic tricks that you can teach your puppy whether you are inside the house or out in the park, such as the following:

Stay
- Speak
- Bow
- Paw
- Wave
- High Five
- Lay Down
- Play Dead

- Roll Over
- Crawl
- Fetch

Stay- When you are taking your puppy out with you to the park or the mall, this trick is important for your puppy to know. To stay is to behave, and it denotes discipline, especially in places where there are many people and many things that could distract your puppy. Some untrained puppies would just go right ahead and run around sniffing things. Knowing the trick or command of staying means your puppy would stay in place and just sit beside you while you wait in line, for example, at the mall, or when you're talking to someone at the park and need to stop walking for a few minutes.

This is also useful even in simpler situations like when you are playing hide and seek, and you still have to hide an item for him to find; teaching him to stay could give you some time. To execute, simply make your puppy sit. Hold a dog  treat in front of him or her and say "Stay." Move backwards slowly all the while saying "Good boy/girl" in a praising tone if he/she remains sitting in his/her place. Start with a few steps, and then you may go inside the house or the other side of the yard. Give your puppy the dog treat when you return to him/her.

Speak- When you tell your puppy, "Speak," he or she will start barking. This trick is useful for your puppy to learn especially in cases of emergencies. If your puppy knows how to bark on command, he/she can alert other people to open the gate for you or to call other people to help you when the need arises. This isn't quite a difficult trick to teach. When your puppy is barking at something, simply say, "Speak," and give him a treat when he barks at your command. Shortly thereafter, your puppy would know that you want him/her to bark whenever you say speak.

Bow- Some masters like to playfully fight with their puppies and would like to teach their puppies to bow before they fight so that they would look like karate opponents. To make your puppy bow is to put him in a position that is similar to when he/she stretches in the morning. His/her chest or whole upper body is lowered on the ground with his/her front legs reaching forward, and his/her rear end pointing up to the air. This trick is also a nice way to make your puppy show respect for someone. The goal is to make your puppy bow at your command.

To execute, start when your puppy is standing on all his/her four legs. Say "Bow" and gently push his/her upper body part down to the ground. Try to see if your puppy can do it on his/her own the next time you say bow. If he/she does, give him/her a treat.

Paw- This trick is very common to puppies and older dogs alike. Masters like teaching this trick to their puppies as their gesture of greeting not just each other, but also when the master would like his/her puppy to meet other people. It is also a good way of showing others that your puppy is well-mannered. This is simply like shaking hands.

To give it a try, stretch a hand in front of him above his front leg and say, "Paw" or "Shake" while you hold out a treat in front of him just slightly above his nose with your other hand. Take one of his/her paws and shake hands with him/her. Tell your puppy that he/she is a good boy/girl right after doing so and give him/her the treat. The next time you say paw or shake, your puppy will reach out to you.

Wave- One of the fun things about teaching tricks to your puppy is that one trick can lead to another. For instance, the paw trick can lead to a variety, such as this one: the wave. This is also good for greeting people, and the kids especially find this amazing. Remember to be enthusiastic when teaching tricks to your puppy and be sure to let them know that he/she is doing a good job.

The wave is just like the paw trick. Make your puppy sit down in front of you. You reach out to your puppy with one hand and hold out a dog treat just a few inches from his/her nose with your other hand. Once your puppy starts to lift his/her paw, pull it back to make your puppy wave and just say, "Wave". Praise him/her cheerily after doing so and reward him/her with a treat.

High Five- Another variety of the paw trick is the high five. Kids are also very fond of seeing puppies do this trick. Start with your puppy sitting down and do at least two paw exercises to warm him/her up. Again, one hand should be reaching out to your puppy and the other should be holding out a treat for him/her. And then, on the third paw exercise, as your puppy raises his/her hands to give you a paw, open your palms with your fingers pointing up and ever so lightly slap with his/hers—this way, you are now palm to paw. Say "high five" and give him a treat. If your puppy becomes confused by the instructions, lower your hand and teach him a low five instead. Don't forget to give your puppy a treat. This way, he/she would know if he/she is able to keep up with what you want him/her to achieve.

Lay Down- Like the paw trick, the lay down trick is like a starting position that leads to yet another set of other tricks. This is useful especially when you are going out with your puppy. A well-behaved puppy is worthy of praise. As you may have noticed, in some malls, they acquire a team of security personnel with canine units which are usually German Shepherds. These big dogs, no matter the crowd that can build up in a mall, remain calm. They just lay down on the floor until commanded to do otherwise.

Your puppy can also be this well-behaved without having to pay much to get the training. This trick will basically make your puppy lie down with his stomach flat on the ground and his front paws stretching out. The proven most effective way of executing this is by having your puppy sit down first then say, "Lay down." Hold up the treat in your hand in front of your puppy and lower your hand to the ground. The tendency is for your puppy to follow the gesture of hand which is to lie down because of the doggy treat. Remember to be firm with your puppy; give him/her the food only when he/she has done the trick correctly. Once he/she does so, praise your puppy enthusiastically for encouragement.

Play Dead- This is one of everybody's favorite tricks to see. Playing dead is a fun way to get people excited about your puppy. You start with easier commands to warm your puppy up such as sit and lie down. Once in the laying position, you point to your puppy with your fingers in the form of a gun and say, "Bang!" then gently roll your puppy to his side. After this, allow your puppy to sit again, praise him/her enthusiastically and reward him/her with a treat. You may repeat this a few times until your puppy gets the idea that he/she is supposed to do a half roll on one side whenever you say bang. Don't forget to give your puppy a dog treat for every correct execution.

Roll over- This is one of the oldest tricks in the book and everybody likes to see their pet puppies do it. It is important that you have taught your puppy the lay down trick because it will make it easier for him/her to start from there. Start by having your puppy sit down and lay down. Once your puppy is in his/her lay down position, simply say, "Roll over" and gently roll your puppy's body from one side to the other. It's just like playing dead but this time, your puppy must do a complete roll and not just on one side. Once he/she completes a roll, give your puppy a treat.

Another way of executing or teaching this trick to your puppy is by using the power of the doggy treat throughout the process. Scratch your puppy playfully until he/she is in a lay down position, then with one hand hold a dog treat and let it pass his/her nose, chin, and one ear to the other by circling around the back of his neck. Say, "Roll over" while doing this. Your puppy will be tracing the movement of the doggy treat around him and as a result, your puppy will fall over from one side to another and back to his lay down position again. Give your puppy the treat after he/she has completed a roll.

Crawl- For masters who have kids in the house who practically grow up together, this is one of kids' favorite tricks to do with the puppies. To crawl is to move forward while in a lay down position. Start off by having your puppy in a lay down position. Say "Crawl" while you move a treat a few inches from your puppy's nose and start moving it away slowly. Your puppy will follow his/her treat while crawling. Some puppy owners like to add little props while teaching this trick, making their pet go through a game of "how low can you go?" as the puppy crawls under the limbo line. Don't forget to give your puppy his/her treat when he/she starts to do the trick, even if he/she moves just a few steps away. This will let your puppy know that doing such a thing rewards him/her with a treat.

Fetch- Lastly on this list of examples of tricks to teach your puppy is fetching. As already mentioned before, fetch is the act of retrieving something that you threw. Not all puppies would understand right away that you want them to get the ball or stick for you. Puppy owners often play this game with their pets. Aside from a stick, and a ball, a Frisbee is also very common when playing this game with puppies and older dogs.

It's part of your puppy's nature to run after things that are thrown away by their masters; the tricky part here is to have your puppy be trained and disciplined enough to bring back to you what you have thrown away. To execute, try throwing an item away from you. Make sure that your puppy is beside you when you do this. Point to the item and say with enthusiasm, "Fetch boy/girl." When your puppy grabs the item with his mouth, call him/her back to you. You can do so by patting your lap and signaling him/her to come to you. While he/she moves closer back to where you are, begin to praise him and say things like, "Good boy/girl!" but do not give your puppy a doggy treat before he/she hands you the item. If in any case, your puppy doesn't respond when you throw the item away, begin again.

As you may have noticed, all these tricks that you can teach to your puppies must be accompanied with a treat and you must praise them enthusiastically. These are necessary for your puppy to know that they are doing something good. In the same way, firmly refuse to give your puppies a treat when they make a wrong move or fail to follow instructions. It is also important that you remain patient with them. Like how little kids when they are only beginning to learn, all these things are new to them and they need to take their time to progress.

Puppies ought to feel that you, as their owner, are supportive of them. No matter how small the amount of their progress is, be there to cheer them on. The truth is that puppies are very sensitive and they can love you so much that they wish to make you proud. At the end of every training session, make them feel that you appreciate their efforts to learn new lessons every day. Your simple body language, hand gestures, and tone of voice can have huge effects on them. Show your support for your puppies by rubbing their tummies, patting their heads, or brushing their fur with your finger. All these little things mean a lot to your puppies.

At the end of the day, remind yourself of the purpose of training and teaching them in the first place. It is not just to impress the people at the mall or at the park that you have such a well-behaved, well-mannered, and well-trained pet. You are engaging yourself and your puppy in this sort of trainings and teachings so that you can spend some quality time together, learning new things and having fun at the same time.

Also, as you go along your trick lessons, make mental notes of how your puppy responds to certain situations. Is your puppy easily distracted? If so, what distracts your puppy the most? Asking yourself such questions can better equip you for your next lessons. The entire point of teaching tricks to your puppy is to have a better relationship with him/her. Teaching them one trick every day can not only improve their mental and physical health, but yours as well. At the end of it all, it gives both of you enough time to grow even closer with each other.

Chapter 10 – The Ultimate Guide to Stop Biting And Mouthing

Biting and mouthing are unacceptable behaviors, whether for a puppy or an adult dog. These are destructive and harmful behaviors that can ruin your furniture and other possessions. Dog bites are no fun—both for the owner and for others.

Most puppies tend to bite during play and when they are in the teething stage. A lot of owners do nothing about this until later, when the adult dog starts biting other people. It is very important to curb this behavior early on to prevent problems in the future.

Why puppies bite

A puppy is in a stage where he first learns about the things around him. Everything is new and exciting. The natural instinct is to explore, to try to find out more about the world where he lives. To do this, a puppy relies with his mouth. He does not have any hands to hold things and manipulate them. What he conveniently has is his mouth. Most of the learning he gets through biting. He finds out if something is food by taking a bite. He learns if something can be played with by biting and shaking it. So basically, a puppy bites to learn more about something. This is natural behavior. What makes it unnatural, destructive and unsafe is when the puppy grows older and uses biting for something else. A dog will bite anything and anyone when he does not learn how to control the behavior. This is why responsible owners should adequately teach their dogs how to control biting.

To start, puppies do not yet understand or realize how strong their bites are and its effects. Bites are also part of their play-fighting behaviors. Play-fighting is important in a puppy's life because it is a part of his learning process. He develops his reflexes, physical skills and coordination. It is also one of the most basic forms of socialization for a puppy. It teaches them socialization skills, how they can and should interact with others.

Bite inhibition is very important for a puppy to learn. This is learning to control how much force to put on biting. This also helps to make them less aggressive and more obedient.

How to Stop Biting Behaviors

You have to teach your puppy to stop biting before they reach 4 months of age to be fully successful. Biting behaviors are learned from the dog's mother, other member of the pack and among the litter during the 1st 4 months of a puppy's life.

For larger dog breeds, a puppy is already too large at 4 months and harder to control. Most children would be uncomfortable playing with a large puppy. Hence, you should start socialization before a puppy is 4 months old.

Most puppies are already taken from the litter before this age. The learning is not yet complete and the puppy will turn to you for the continuance of his training. When you teach him not to bite during this crucial period, you will most likely be successful.

Trust and Respect

Establishing a trusting and mutually respective relationship can control biting behaviors. Teach your puppy to trust you by providing for all his needs. Feed him on time and treat him when he is sick or hurt. Make him feel loved and well protected.

As has been explained in previous chapters, a puppy that respects his owner will be obedient. When he does, it will be much easier to get your puppy to listen to you as you teach him to stop biting.

Socialization

Inadequate socialization is a major reason why puppies grow up to be biting dogs. They become aggressive because they are not used to being around others. They are uncomfortable, even fearful. When dogs are afraid, they either run away or bite. Also, puppies that are not used to being around children also tend to bite them.

Getting your puppy to socialize more is one step to inhibit biting behaviors. Have your puppy interact with friendly and well socialized dogs. The learning process continues as your puppy learns social behaviors from these well trained dogs.

Puppies naturally tumble, play and roll with each other. In the course of their play, they bite each other. Your puppy will learn to control biting urges when they play with other dogs that have already learned control.

Your puppy will learn if he is playing too rough through the reactions of his playmates. This is a natural process that you should allow in order to teach biting control. You have to realize that this learning process is something your puppy has to naturally undergo. It is only learned through trial and error during his interactions with other dogs.

Socialization will not only help in teaching your puppy to control his biting. It also helps your puppy to release his energy in a more acceptable manner. Puppies have lots of energy. They are like little balls of fur with inexhaustible energy. By letting them play with other dogs, some of the energies are released. This also helps to keep them physically and mentally healthy. A puppy that has too much energy and does not get to play turns into a destructive and hyperactive pet in the home.

By letting your puppy play with other dogs, he does not have to treat you and your family as his littermates. That means he will be less inclined to play-bite you. Over time, he will learn not to associate humans with biting.

Also, through socialization, your puppy will be more comfortable around other dogs. They will not be fearful and will be less inclined to be aggressive or bite.

Reprimands

Teach your puppy to associate biting to negative reinforcements. When bites during your play, tell him in a firm but gentle voice "Stop". Then ignore him for a few minutes, about 15-20.

However, avoid harsh reprimands such as slapping, hitting or kicking. Harsh punishments will quickly destroy any trust he has in you. And he is much less likely to listen and obey you when he no longer trusts and respects you.

When you reprimand your puppy, make sure to follow it up after a few minutes. Do not wait too long because the window for learning is only limited. When you reprimand, you ignore for 15-20 minutes. After this, make it up with another round of play or other pleasurable activities. This way, your puppy will come to understand that the reprimand was for the biting and not because you no longer like him.

Be consistent. Reprimand your puppy each time he bites. He will not learn biting control if you deal with the issue inconsistently.

Recognize that reprimanding alone will not effectively teach your puppy to stop biting. You have to reinforce the teaching with other methods.

Use Mother Dog's Training Technique

Mother dogs are naturally very efficient in keeping their litter in line. She is the one puppies learn their behaviors from. Puppies also naturally follow and obey what their mother tells them to do. There is no one more perfect to pattern training techniques than her. Respected trainers have long been using a mother dog's technique as a pattern for puppy training.

To start, understand what and how a mother dog keeps order and discipline within her brood. She lets her puppies play with her. They tumble, roll, play-fight and occasionally gnaw or bite each other. She even lets her puppies practice their bite strength on her. When the puppies bite too hard, she growls. It is the equivalent of a human "Ouch!" or "Stop". When the mother dog yelps, the puppies are surprised. Unsure of what this means and what to do, the puppies take a step back and look at their mother. Their mother ignores them. Hesitantly, the puppies try to bite her again to see if it has something to do with it. When the puppies bite her again, she yelps louder than before. She faces the biting puppy, shows her teeth and growls. This behavior is the equivalent of a human scolding. After this, she turns around and walks away. The puppies would naturally follow her but she continues to ignore the biting puppy. This is sending a message that the puppy bit too hard and the behavior is unacceptable. Some puppies take a few more lessons before the message becomes clear. The mother dog consistently reacts this way, to each of her brood, until they all eventually get the lesson she is trying to teach.

If the puppy continues to bite hard despite the scowling and growling, she uses a higher level of reprimand. She grabs the offending puppy by the scruff of the neck and shakes him firmly. If the puppy struggles or fights back, she gives him another good shake, often more vigorous than the first. It is like telling the puppy not to "talk back" when she scolds him. She only puts the puppy down when he shows signs of contriteness and submission. The puppy relaxes, keeps still and flattens his ears back against his head. For more aggressive puppies, she pins them to the ground, angrily growls at them and nips at the puppies with her teeth. The goal is to threaten them but not to really hurt them. She keeps them pinned until they show signs of submission. When she releases them, the puppies would shake their fur off and then look for another playmate or do another activity.

You do not have to do the growling thing or shaking the puppy with your teeth. But, most of the mother dog's behaviors are highly recommended. When the puppy bites you during play, yelp or say "Ouch!" This will jolt their attention to you and away from the play activity. Do so in a high-pitched voice. Dog can hear high-pitched sounds better. Exaggerate your reaction a bit, just to show your puppy that you are hurt by his biting. Refuse to play, even if he approaches and tries to engage you. Ignore him for a few minutes to let the message sink in. if he continues to bite or attempts to bite again, yelp again and hold him by the scruff. Give a little but firm shake. Scold him using a lower voice tone. Use your threatening voice for this, to exaggerate the scolding a bit. This is just to show him that you mean business. If the puppy continues with the biting behavior and does not learn the lesson you are trying to teach, take the training up one notch. The next time he bites, yelp and flip him on his back. Scold them again in a threatening, low-pitched voice while keeping them pinned down. Release the puppy only when you feel his body relaxing, he is not looking directly in your eyes, and he shows no signs of aggression.

Choosing games

The games you let your puppy play are also very important determining factors. Games like tug of war and wrestling are confusing games for him. These games involve a few biting. These make it harder for your puppy to recognize what is acceptable biting o=and what is not. It is best to avoid these.

Chapter 11 – The Ultimate Guide In Puppy Advanced Training

In this chapter, you will learn:

1. The Different Types Of Puppy Advanced Training
   a. Agility Training
   b. Canine Good Citizen Training
   c. Top Dog Sport
   d. Therapy Dogs And Animal-Assisted Therapy
   e. Service Dogs
   f. Actor Dogs
2. Fading Or Gradually Removing The Prompts And Lures

Training your puppy is an ongoing and a lifetime process. There would always be room for improvement. Nobody can claim that his dog has mastered everything and that there is no more need to learn and train. It is vital that you keep working with your puppy with those things he has learned throughout his lifetime.

The "use it or lose it" saying can also be applied to your puppy's trainings. He can forget some of those commands or tricks if you do not remind him from time to time. Plus, this is also a great way to have quality time with your puppy. What's more, continuous training of new skills and tricks would stimulate your puppy to keep growing and maturing emotionally, socially, and even mentally.

The Different Types Of Puppy Advanced Training

When your puppy has accomplished the basic training, it is time to bring him up to the next level, which is the advanced training. This would also provide physical and mental stimulation for him, turning him into a more matured and responsible dog. There are different courses that you can take. Again, base your decision on what course to give your dog according to his breed and personality and according to your needs. Here are your options for advanced training:

> Agility training. This training will improve his accuracy and speed in performing some tasks. If you want your puppy to join in canine sports competitions, then this training is a must for him. A more detailed discussion of this type of training can be found in the next chapter.

> Canine good citizen training. This is a two-part program designed to achieve the following:
>   o Responsible pet ownership for owners, and
>   o Basic good manners for dogs — whether inside the home or outside, with owners or with strangers.

> Top Dog Sports. Aside from the obstacle course to be overcome in agility training, there are other contests and sports that you can enroll your puppy in.

> Therapy Dogs and Animal-Assisted Therapy. These dogs facilitate recovery for people with various ailments. Their main goal is to provide hope and inspiration plus lifting up the spirits of the physically and emotionally hurting individuals.

> Service Dogs or Vocational Training. This is teaching a wide variety of skills that would benefit other people such as search and rescue work, and police dog work

and support/assist work with physically challenged individuals.

> ➢ Actor Dogs. Do you want to see your puppy on television? Then this training is for him to learn the dos and don'ts of becoming an actor.

Dogs, just like human beings, can assume different roles. Some could be the source of a family's fun and love. Other dogs could be the source of pride of their owners when they win in competitions. Still some could help augment the income of their owners when they work as dog actors. And yes, there are dogs that can be trained to protect and save lives. It is undeniable how precious these pets are to their owners.

To get the most of your puppy, training him is of utmost importance. Training takes place the moment the puppy is born or brought to your house. There are different levels of training. In the previous chapters, all the basic trainings needed were already tackled. In this chapter, the advanced level will be the focus of discussion.

As mentioned, a whole chapter for agility training is provided. Here are the rest of the advanced training courses that you can choose for your puppy. Remember to assess what would be the ideal advanced course for your puppy based on his personality and breed. It would also depend on what you need for him to do — for instance, provide protection for the house (as a guard dog) or be a form of transport (sled dog).

Canine Good Citizen Training

Puppy Training Guide 4th Edition

Dogs can earn a Canine Good Citizen certificate when they pass the test being administered. This certificate is sometimes required for some training, especially in advanced obedience training such as dog sports or therapy dogs. The test consists of 10 skills or behaviors that the dog needs to perform without growling, barking, or snapping. Foods and treats are not allowed during the test, too.

To pass the test, your puppy must be able to do the following:

1. The dog remains calm while a complete stranger approaches you and stops to talk to you.
2. The dog should remain calm while a stranger comes over him and pets him.
3. The dog would be handled the same way he is being handled during grooming or an exam. While being handled in such a manner, he should accept it and not resist it.
4. The dog should be able to walk calmly, without pulling or lunging, when on a loose leash.
5. The dog should be calm while he walks though a crowd on a loose leash.
6. You dog can perform the "sit," "stay," and "down" commands.
7. The dog should come when his name is called.
8. The dog should remain calm when another dog and his handler are approaching.
9. He should not be distracted and must manifest calmness even when loud noises are presented.
10. Your dog should remain calm even when you give his leash to another person and you walk away.

Top Dog Sports

Nowadays, there are many types of dog sports and recreation that you can enroll your puppy in. These sports would not only bring your "man-canine bond" to a higher and more intimate level but it would also improve your dog's physical and mental attributes.

Choose which best fits your puppy. Here are some of your choices:

Canine Freestyle. Do you know that dogs can "dance?" This is basically what canine freestyle is! It is a choreographed musical performance wherein the handler and the puppy would do steps or moves similar to dancing. Some of the routine moves are walking backward, jumping, twisting and turning, and weaving through the handler's legs.

Disc Dogs. Like Frisbee, disc dogs is a sport wherein the handler would throw a disc and the dog must catch it. The event is scored based on the following criteria: distance, accuracy of the catch, and freestyle routines. In the actual competition, the field is divided into zones by yards. A corresponding score is given to the specific zone where the dog caught the disc.

Conformation. In here, purebreds are presented and judged according to congruity or conformity with their respective breed standards. The dog should display the ideal physical characteristics, temperament, and gait as expected by their breed. Winners of these competitions are in demand for breeding and their offspring are priced higher than non-winners.

Dock Diving or Dock Jumping. In this competition, the dogs jump as high and as far as possible from a dock right into a body of water. The basis of the distance covered is where the tail base touches the water. Jumps are recorded digitally to ensure accurate and fair measurement.

Lure Coursing. It is a fast-paced sport with the goal of feeding the chasing instinct of the dog, in the safest and most humane way possible. In lure coursing, an artificial lure is used to compete for the best time that the dog will catch the lure. There are instances in this sport that obstacles are set up across the field to make the competition even more challenging.

Rally Obedience. In this event, there are specific obedience exercises that the dog must be able to perform. The judges are the ones that designed the course. The handler/dog team should be able to navigate swiftly and completely through the course.

Tracking. This is like a simulation of the search-and-rescue work in real life. The dog must be able to track a scent in the least possible time. This could be a way to determine if your puppy is also suitable as a service dog.

Flyball. This is a relay race involving four dogs. The dogs are released one by one. The flyball sport includes running down a course, jumping through hurdles, and going to the "flyball box" to get a tennis ball. Once the tennis ball is with the dog, he returns to the starting line to give the ball to his handler while another dog is released to do the same thing. The first team to complete this exercise wins.

Herding Trials. To herd a group of animals is an instinct for a dog. Since most dogs live in the urban areas, this instinct is suppressed. This is one of the most enjoyable sports for dogs.

There are other sports, competitions, and activities that you and your dog can join. Check online or through any of the dog organizations or clubs in your area.

Therapy Dogs and Animal-Assisted Therapy (AAT)

The use of therapy dogs to treat ailments or diseases that are physical, social, emotional, and/or cognitive in nature is becoming popular. Why? The link between quick recovery and the participation of animals, specifically dogs, is undeniable. Dogs really provide therapeutic effects to these individuals afflicted with different medical conditions. Children and the elderly, in particular, benefit so much from these therapies involving dogs.

For a dog to qualify as a therapy animal, he would need a certificate from the Canine Good Citizen Training Program (or its equivalent) and a consent letter from his instructor. He should also possess the following characteristics:

> ➢ Good temperament. This is the most important requirement. Some patients are irritable and impatient. The dog, therefore, must possess a good personality,

such as being friendly and non-aggressive, in spite of being with people who are not feeling well, physically and emotionally.

- ➢ Sociable. He must get along with all types of people and animals, especially with little children and the elderly and with other animals that are also around.
- ➢ Gentleness and calm. Patients should be protected from any form of stress. A calm and gentle dog could provide that stress-free atmosphere.

A therapy dog's job is actually light and fun. Depending on the needs of the sick individual, he could simply sit beside the patient and allow himself to be petted. The patients could also take him to a walk, play with him, or feed him. Therapy dogs that have disabilities or limitations can become sources of inspiration and hope for patients, too.

How can your puppy become a therapy dog?

You and your dog becoming a therapy team could be one of the most rewarding experiences the two of you could share. Nothing compares to the joy of being of help to others without expecting anything in return and of being able to give hope, inspiration, and happiness to them in your own little ways. The process may seem long but one thing is for sure — it is worth it.

Start your journey of becoming a therapy team by participating in the Canine Good Citizen Training Program and obtaining a certificate. Completing the program is an indication that your dog is obedient, well-mannered, and sociable. For many therapy dog programs, this certificate is a prerequisite for qualification.

Once you have the certificate, coordinate with an animal-assisted therapy organization officer. Know what you and your dog need to accomplish to become a therapy team. The requirements can vary according to each organization's rules and standards.

As you are going to deal with sick people, the dog must be of good health. Have a veterinarian thoroughly check him up first before he starts being a therapy dog.

Finally, after all the requirements have been completed, there is a series of evaluation that both of you would need to undergo and pass. After that, you can then officially start as a therapy team. This simply means that you can visit hospitals and other facilities and touch these people's lives, just by bringing your dog there.

Service Dogs or Vocational Training

Dogs can totally make a person's life so much better just by being themselves. Just to see their tails wagging or their excited faces upon spotting you could warm your heart. However, they can do more than that. It is not just their cuteness or loveliness that make them man's best friend indeed. It is also their ability to assist man with so many things.

This is where vocational training comes in. Here, your dog can be trained to do things such as the following:

➢ Search-and-rescue work
➢ Assist the disabled
➢ Herd a group of animals
➢ Hunt

- ➢ Protect you and your property
- ➢ Assist law enforcement officers
- ➢ Save lives

There are five main types:

Assistance Dogs. These dogs are trained to provide company to humans with mental or physical disabilities. The goal is for these individuals to have a more independent and productive life. The most popular breed to become an assistance dog is the Labrador Retriever.

Rescue Dogs. You see a lot of movies where they use dogs during searches for missing or lost people. It's not for movies or shows only but these rescue dogs are for real. So many lives have been helped because of the assistance of these dogs. The dog must possess great stamina and intelligence as the work may require lengthy periods of time and harsh environments plus the possibility of danger.

Personal Protection Dogs. This is equivalent to a human bodyguard. The dog's main purpose is to protect people and their homes. They are highly trained, loyal to their owners, intelligent, and strong.

Estate Guard Dogs. Just like a canine bodyguard, their role is to provide protection to family and property. By nature, they are very territorial and rightly so, in order to ward off intruders.

Sled Dogs. These dogs are strong and hardworking. Their main job is to pull sleighs or sleds over ice or snow.

Actor Dogs. They can also be stars, next to Hollywood actors and actresses. These dogs should be able to follow commands while their owners are at a distance. They should also know many tricks and commands. They should be sociable and love to be around people and other animals. After all, those are the traits of real Hollywood stars.

Which is which?

There are so many skills and trainings that your puppy can learn and use for your benefit, as well as for other people's benefit. Depending on your dog's personality and breed, he can even excel in more than one advance training. Be proud of your puppy and of yourself because together, you and your puppy would be able to achieve so much. Your puppy's victory is your victory, too.

Fading Or Gradually Removing The Prompts And Lures

What are prompts?

These are cues or hints that you give your puppy to signal a command. For example, pointing to the floor would precede the cue "down." Tightening the collar is also a prompt. As mentioned, there might be times that you would not be able to do these prompts so your puppy must still learn to obey without these prompts. A food lure is also a prompt.

What are lures?

These are items that you use because your puppy likes these things very much, such as food or toys. For instance, in agility training, you use food to keep the puppy's head down to the plank in teeter-totter. In the actual competition, food would not be allowed. Your puppy's head should be lower with no lures to encourage so. Hence, this training is also a must.

Why do you need to do this?

Imagine your child obeying your commands and requests just because he knows that after following them, you will give him cookies or new toys. That would be disastrous if he is expecting this routine each time you ask him for something. You know that it is not a good thing to teach your child to be like that. The same thing applies for your puppy.

At the beginning of most trainings, you provide treats and words of encouragement to reinforce the behaviors and skills being taught. However, there should come a time that your puppy would still follow your command even if there were no rewards from you. This requires training, too, known as the fading of the prompts and lures.

A lot of owners are guilty of missing out on this training. However, there is really a must to do this early and consistently, both for your sake and your puppy's. This training could save your puppy.

How to do it?

1. First, assess your puppy's obedience with the use of prompts and lures. In the skill "down," for instance, point to the floor (if this is your prompt for him to get down) and see what the puppy would do. Most likely, he would get the prompt and stay down. This time, do not point or do anything but just say "down." It is not

unusual that your puppy will just look at you and continue to wait for instructions. This simply means that it is time to train him. You need to fade the prompts and lures.

2. Reverse the sequence. This time, before you give the cue or action, verbalize your command first. So, using the above example, say "down" and then point to the floor. Do this several times until the puppy realizes that "down" and pointing to the floor are one and the same.

3. Gradually lose the prompt. Try to make the gap wider between the verbal command and the prompt. So if you say "down," wait for a couple of seconds before you point to the floor. This may require several practices. Then, as he gets it more and more, try to lose the prompt gradually, too. For instance, the way you point to the ground is at 6 inches. Next time, point at 12 inches, then at 15 inches, and then, after several successful repetitions, do not point to the floor anymore.

4. With lures, you can also gradually fade or lose them by giving fewer treats each time. Practice until you have reached the level wherein you do not have to give any treat and your puppy still follows your verbal command.

Congratulations! You have reached another level. You should be very proud of yourself and of your puppy.

Chapter 12 – The Ultimate Guide In Puppy Agility Training

In this chapter, you will learn:

1. The Definition Of Agility Training
2. The Types Of Obstacles In Puppy Agility Training
3. The Benefits of Puppy Agility Training
4. DIY Obstacle Course
5. How To Get Started In The Agility Training Of Your Puppy
6. A Step-by-Step Guide In Puppy Agility Training
   a. Pause Table
   b. Pause Box
   c. Tunnel
   d. Weave Poles
   e. Dog walk
   f. A-Frame
   g. Teeter-Totter
   h. Tire Jump
   i. Putting It All Together
7. The Arrays Of Puppy Agility Training

The Definition Of Agility Training

Agility is the ability to move gracefully and quickly. Your puppy can acquire agility through proper training. Wouldn't you like to see your puppy have the skills to pass through tunnels or balance through planks quickly and safely? Wouldn't it also be fun to enter your puppy in agility competitions?

Puppy agility training is coaching your puppy to perform specific tasks and overcome obstacles. This is one good training exercise for active dogs so that their excess energies would be converted into better use. It prevents your puppy from being bored, too. Aside from these, there are other benefits of agility training, both for you and your puppy.

Agility training is also a popular canine sport wherein the dog would be tested and graded based on their ability to complete and overcome set obstacles. In the actual competition (if you do plan to join one soon) remember that there would be no food or treat allowed from the owner or handler. The puppy is also off-leash. Plus, touching the puppy during the competition is not permitted. The puppy must perform all the obstacles as perfectly and as quickly as possible through the handler's voice command or some body language or movement only.

The Types Of Obstacles In Puppy Agility Training

Here are the different types of obstacles used in competition. These may vary depending on the rules and regulations of each Dog Agility Club or Organization.

> ➤ **Tunnel**. This is made up of a vinyl tube with a length of between 10 to 20 feet and a diameter of about 2 feet. The challenge is for the dog to run through the whole tunnel, which is oftentimes configured in a straight line or sometimes in a variety of curves, depending on the requirements of the organizers of the competition. There are other variations of tunnels such as a collapsed tunnel wherein the puppy must pass through a barrel-like cylinder with a chute or cloth (around 8 to 12 feet)

attached to it. The dog must push through the collapsed tube. In addition, there is also the skeleton tunnel. This is very challenging also as there is no cloth covering the tunnel. It means that if the puppy is not disciplined or well-trained enough, he would go out of the tunnel from the side or body of the tunnel.

➤ **Teeter-Totter**. This is like a child's seesaw. A 10- to 12-foot plank is slightly held off-balanced by a fulcrum, making one end of the plank touch the ground all the time. Usually, the plank has a rubberized surface so that it is skid-free for the puppies. The target is for the dog to cross the plank from the beginning side-up to the other side. There is a contact zone here, meaning an area is painted yellow, and the purpose is to make it a safe zone for the dog. The dog should touch the contact zone or else he will be faulted (grades or scores will be deducted) when he misses the contact zone.

➤ **Tire Jump**. It looks exactly like a tire hanging on a frame. The puppy must be able to jump through this "tire." It is covered all over with tape to protect the puppy from any loose ends or uneven places within the "tire." There are new products that would break away or be displaced if the puppy hits the tire in any way to prevent hurting him.

➤ **Weave Poles Obstacle**. Considered as one of the most difficult obstacles to master, the weave poles obstacle has a series of 5 to 12 poles placed in an upright position. The height of the pole is 3 feet each while the space between each pole is 24 inches. The target is for the puppy to pass through the poles, beginning on the one to his left and not to skip any pole, until he reaches the last pole.

> **Pause Table**. There is a square platform with a measurement of 3 feet by 3 feet. The height of the table is from 8 to 30 inches, depending on the height of the puppy and the rules of the competition. The dog must jump on it and stay seated or remain in a down position for a given period of time (usually 5 seconds). A variation of this is the pause box wherein there is a square marked on the ground, either made of construction tape or PVC pipes. Just like the pause table, the puppy needs to sit and stay there until the designated time is up.

> **Standard Jumps**. A horizontal bar hangs from two upright posts. The height of the bar depends on the puppy. The puppy must jump over the bar without hitting it.

> **A-Frame**. Two ramps, about 3 feet wide by 8 feet long, are hinged together in such a way that the hinged connection is placed upright. It gives a shape of the letter A, hence the name. The dog must ascend on one plank and then descend on the other plank. This obstacle has a contact zone, too.

The Benefits Of Puppy Agility Training

Agility training is one of the advanced trainings you can do to your puppy. It is recommended not only for the dog's benefit but for his owner, as well. Here are 7 reasons agility training is good for you and your puppy.

Puppy Training Guide 4th Edition

1. Agility training will satisfy your puppy's natural instincts. Dogs, by nature, enjoy activities such as running, chasing something, jumping, climbing, and squeezing through things. In the obstacles of agility training, all these natural desires and behaviors would be fulfilled. The obstacles are designed in such a way that they mimic the actual activities of dogs when they are in the wild. It brings out the natural instincts in them. So for owners, do not worry that your dogs might find the training difficult. They are actually enjoying the training.

2. They make your puppy stronger physically. Exercise is good for your puppy. This training will provide many opportunities for your puppy to stretch and strengthen those muscles and improve his speed. This will also enhance coordination of different body parts. In addition, there would be increased endurance. Agility training gets your puppy into shape while he is having fun.

3. In agility training, there is also mental stimulation. The puppy needs to use his intellect and instincts to pass through the obstacles. Sometimes, his decision-making skill is put to the test especially since there would be no tactile assistance to be given to him by his owner or handler during the competition.

4. It increases his confidence in himself and in his ability. The puppy knows that he has achieved something major, just by learning and overcoming the obstacles, regardless whether he joins and wins in the competition or not.

5. It improves the puppy's personality. A shy dog will become bolder while an aggressive dog will become more sociable with agility training. You will have a happier and a healthier dog.

6. It fosters a better relationship between the puppy and the owner. Agility training requires complete dependence of your dog on you, as the handler. The obstacles are designed in such a way that your dog would be able to complete the tasks only through obedience and reliance on you. To achieve this, your dog must trust you 100% and you should have confidence in your dog's capabilities 100%, too. This training will therefore improve communication between yourself and your puppy. Plus, in the process, your puppy's obedience will improve and positive behaviors will be reinforced even when he is outside the agility course.

7. It will improve your physical health, too. As you run and train with your puppy, you would also benefit from the physical workout that goes with it.

DIY Obstacle Course

You can set up your own agility course at your backyard to prepare the puppy for agility competition or just for the fun of it. Here is how you can do it yourself.

➢ *Weave poles.* Just stick 10 to 15 PVC pipes into the ground (or find other materials that would do). Follow the recommended spacing of each stick, which is at 24 inches apart. If your backyard is too small to accommodate the space requirement, you could do it at

22 inches apart with fewer sticks, provided that your puppy is comfortable with it. You can also buy the orange traffic cone if you do not want to stick anything on your ground, especially if it is landscaped.

> *Standard jump.* Stack 2 cinder blocks and place a strip of plywood across them. Measure the height of your puppy so that the jump would be appropriate for him.

> *Pause table.* Any table that is low and stable enough can be utilized for this exercise. For the pause box, simply use construction tape and create a 3-feet by 3-feet square mark on the ground.

> *Dog walk.* This time, use the cinder blocks and place a 12-foot piece of plywood across them. You can also use a park bench or picnic bench to train your puppy to do this exercise. In the actual competition, this will have a contact zone so paint that yellow.

> *Tunnel.* A child's collapsible tunnel can be used instead. However, if you can find something that is light and yet has enough weight to remain upright when your puppy passes through it, all the the better. Passing through a tunnel might seem scary for a little dog so try to make it as much fun as possible. Look for a tunnel that can be scrunched or shortened. This way, the training is gradual and by the time the puppy needs to cover the entire length of the tunnel, he is already past the fear of passing it.

> *Tire Jump.* The old tires of bikes or cars can be strung to a sturdy tree. That would be the jump tire for your puppy. Just make sure that the diameter of the tire is large enough for the puppy's body to pass through safely. Also, hang the tire in such a way that it is ideal to

the height of the puppy. Another good alternative is a child's Hula-Hoop, although the diameter of this is sometimes too wide to make a good practice tire jump.

➤ *Teeter-Totter boards.* Use some PVC pipes (as the base) and a long piece of wood (as the board). Apply anti-skid to the paint and cover the board with this mixture. This will give more traction as your puppy walks across it. Again, don't forget the contact zone.

It is not necessary to have all the obstacles set up in your backyard, unless you really have a large backyard. Just choose to set up what you think is appropriate for your puppy and you. However, if you do plan to enter your puppy into a real competition, then either completing the obstacle course or enrolling your puppy in a class would be the better option.

How To Get Started In The Agility Training Of Your Puppy

Here are the general guidelines to observe when starting to train your puppy for agility.

1. Remember that not all puppies are the same. Some are very good at agility training while others can find this very difficult. Hence, a thorough assessment of your puppy's personality according to breed is one important factor to consider. If you think that this is not your puppy's cup of tea, then make an improvised agility course and just have fun with it. Instead of a serious training ground, it could be like a playground for your puppy. However, if your puppy matches the requirements needed to qualify and win in a competition, then by all means, start the training

during the recommended age. The required age is dogs below 9 months (because 0-9 months is too young for such a serious training) and those more than 8 years old (the activities could be too tiring for their age).

2. Bring your puppy to his veterinarian first for a thorough pre-screening checkup. Let his heart, lungs, joints, and eyes be checked since these are of utmost importance during the training. Also, weigh the puppy. As much as possible, he should have the ideal weight before the training or else that extra weight could hinder his performance during practices.

3. Be ready and patient. The complete training could take 6 to 9 months. When your puppy is still too young, teach him impulse control and obedience techniques first. These are prerequisites for the agility training. The puppy should have mastery of simple commands such as "sit," "stay," "lie down," "crawl," "come," "settle," and "jump."

4. Be generous with positive words and treats when you are training. This will give encouragement to your puppy.

5. As the new saying goes, "Practice makes perfect." Teach the right techniques early on. It would be more difficult to "unlearn" learned tricks later on.

6. Name all the obstacles so that the puppy will know which obstacle you are referring to. Remember, only voice commands and some body language will be allowed during the actual competition. When doing the sequencing or how the course will run through, the puppy should know what to do next when he hears your command. For example, the cue for "tunnel" could be "tunnel" or "jump" for jump unless you have another preference for calling them. This type of naming, though, will be easier on your part, too. You could not

afford to make a mistake in cueing during the actual competition.

7. Start the training with safety and mastery of the skill as the focus. Ensure that the puppy will be free from any harm or injury. When these two are accomplished, your next focus is on speed.

8. Make it more fun and interesting both for you and your puppy by joining a support group. See if there is a puppy or dog agility club in your community. This is where you can ask for good trainers too, in case you are looking for one.

9. Do not forget the contact zone. Missing contact zones can be a habit if not dealt with early in the training. At first, you can use wire hoops, chicken wire mesh, or the orange cones to mark the contact zones better. You can also use the technique "Target." This is having your puppy to stop at the bottom of the contact zone. Give him a treat when he stops at the contact zone.

10. The most important guideline is this: make it fun for you and your puppy. Your main target here is not to bring home the trophy. Agility training is about creating and developing that special bond between you and your puppy.

A Step-by-Step Guide In Puppy Agility Training

Start with the safest and most enjoyable obstacle for your puppy. When he has mastered a certain obstacle, you can then proceed with the more challenging one until he completes the whole course.

Pause table. This is just a reinforcement of the Sit-Stay cue that your puppy should have learned during the impulse control training. After running for a while, teaching your puppy to do the pause table may seem like an unwelcome interruption for him. However, this will further enhance his control over impulsivity. The requirement is simple — the puppy must get on the table and sit and stay there for 5 seconds.

Start with a low table. This is to eliminate any fear of heights your puppy may have. While holding his leash, go to the table and give a cue like "table" or "top" and then tap the table. Do not use the cue "jump" as this might confuse him later on. When he jumps on the table, immediately give him a treat to reinforce the action. Spend several seconds praising and loving him. Repeat the exercise for a couple of times.

Next, do the above exercise but let him sit still and count for 5 seconds. Then, give another cue like "okay" or "let's go" to signal that he can go down the table now. You might also want to train him to lie down as some organizations might require that.

Then, if he is used to this exercise, practice this activity again but this time, you should be standing away from the table. The puppy should be able to get on top of the table, stay and sit or lie down for 5 seconds and then get out of the table according to your cues from afar. Finally, when he has mastery of this exercise, start adding height to the table until the required height is reached.

Pause Box. It is very similar to the pause table except that your puppy has to stay and sit inside a square made from pipes laid on the ground. His feet should be within the boundary to pass the obstacle. The cue "tuck" might be helpful for this test. Follow the instructions for the pause table obstacle.

Tunnel. If the tunnel can be shortened, then put it at the shortest length. Put a long leash on your puppy. Find another person to assist you if possible. Let your friend hold the puppy on one end of the tunnel while you bring the leash inside the tunnel on the other end. While you are calling your puppy's name, gently pull the leash toward you, guiding your dog to walk through the tunnel. Reach out your hand with a treat on it so that will motivate him to move to you. Note: Do not put food inside the tunnel as your puppy might get used to pausing and looking for treats while in the tunnel.

When your puppy reaches you, give him a warm hug and lots of praises plus a treat. Repeat the exercise for a few times. The next challenge is to let him go to the tunnel on his own while you are running along with him outside the tunnel, talking and encouraging your puppy at the same time.

When the puppy is used to this exercise, you can now add length to the tunnel. Later on, you could even make a curve (left and right) to make it a more taxing exercise.

Weave Poles. As mentioned, this is one of the hardest skills to master. There are many techniques or methods to do this exercise. The key is not to rush the process of acquiring this skill.

The simplest and cheapest method is to start with 6 poles, with you and your dog on a leash going through the poles. Guide him using your legs and other body language. For every pole, give him a treat and lots of praises.

Here are the other methods to learn how to weave poles.

> ➢ Wire Method. Make a channel path by clipping wires on the poles. Make sure that the wire will not permit the

puppy to go over or under it. When the dog gets the hang of it, you can gradually remove the wire.

> Chute method. Use chicken wire mesh as a channel path. The principle is the same as that of the wire method.
> Channel method. It is a special weave set. The puppy will sort of run through a straight channel (there is no weaving yet). When you move the pole at the center, then a weaving channel is created and the puppy will start to weave just a little. Do this until the puppy learns weaving.
> Slanted pole. Basically, this is just like the channel method. The puppy begins without weaving and when you pull the two poles together, the weaving starts.

Add a pole each time that your puppy is getting better. Do not be frustrated when your puppy's weave poles skill seems to be like that of a yo-yo. It is but normal that sometimes a dog would do really well in one practice and then the next day, he would fail. Just go back to the start of the training until he gets the hang of it. Again, lots of patience is a must here.

Never forget to be appreciative of your puppy's victories (no matter how simple or small they are) and of course, always remember to hand him the treats.

Dog Walk. The plank should be placed at the lowest height possible. Later on, when your puppy is comfortable with the skill, you can add height to the plank. If there is a friend who could help you and your puppy learn this skill, the better.

Tighten your hold on the leash but make sure that your puppy is comfortable. Your friend should stay on the other side of the dog while you start to walk him on the plank. The dog's focus must be on the plank. You can control this by placing your hand and your treat near the plank.

Again, this is a contact obstacle so make sure that the puppy touches the contact zone. Most of the errors occur when the dog jumps off the plank without touching the contact zone.

A-Frame. Start with a low incline first. When your puppy is more confident with the height, you can raise it a little bit until you finally reached the required height. The topmost priority here is the safety of the dog. Also, your puppy should not forget to touch the yellow contact zones at the beginning and bottom of the plank.

If a friend can assist you in this, ask him or her to stay on the other side of the puppy and give him encouragement and praises. Your friend's presence will also lessen your puppy's fears or apprehensions. Hold the leash and assist your puppy in going up. Do it slowly and carefully. While descending, the puppy's tendency is to increase speed or jump off the plank. Continue to hold the leash and just guide him slowly, pausing in the contact zone. Give him treats for every followed cue.

When he is already comfortable on the A-frame plank, you can adjust the height according to the required height.

Teeter-Totter. It would be better if you have a friend (much better if you have 2 friends) to help you. This is one the most difficult obstacles to learn. Your friend should stand on the other side of the puppy. If there is another one, you could ask him or her to hold the plank and be the one to adjust the movement of the plank. Your role is to hold the leash near the neck of the puppy. His head should be low or near the plank. You could do this by putting a treat near the plank. When you reach the middle part where the plank would fall to the other end, your friend can help by preventing the fall to happen too fast. Allow the dog to take tiny steps while the plank slowly goes down.

When the dog is used to this exercise, he will be the one to control the pivot and not anybody else anymore. What to avoid: the fly-offs. This is where your dog jumps off the plank into the ground even before the plank hits the ground. Do not forget to train him to do the contact zone tip, too.

Tire Jump. Start training your puppy to jump over an object with no opening (like in a regular or bar jump) or broad opening (like a hula hoop). The dog can get intimidated with the small diameter of the tire.

Start low. Place the tire on the ground at first. Tap the tire inside. That is your cue for the dog to pass through the tire. If you have a friend with you, ask him to hold the tire while you carry your puppy and pass him through the tire. When his fear of the tire's diameter has been overcome, then let the puppy jump by himself while you wait on the other side of tire, cheering him on. Of course, there should be a corresponding treat, too.

Greet him happily to make learning fun. Start raising the height of the tire. If at anytime your dog goes under the tire, do not give him a treat. When you are adjusting the tire and he went underneath, do not give a treat but lower the tire back to where he was last comfortable. Start the process again.

If your puppy has mastery of this skill already, never go back to lowering the tire's height again as this might hurt your puppy when he miscalculates the height.

Putting It Together

When all the obstacles are familiar to your puppy already, it is time to put the act together. This is known as sequencing. The task that you need to teach your puppy is the order of the obstacles. Do it by two. For instance, jump and tunnel. Give the cue "jump" and even before he has finished the task, tell him the cue for "tunnel" or whatever you named it. The most important thing here is timing. If you give it too late, the puppy might decide by himself what to do next.

When he is comfortable with two obstacles in a row, add another one. Let him practice until he completes the three obstacles. Afterward, add another obstacle until he completes the entire course. If you are satisfied with the timing and speed, then you and your puppy are ready for the real thing — a real competition!

The Different Arrays Of Puppy Agility Training

There is an order of arrangement for agility training according to the skill of the puppy. This array can vary according to the rules per organization. Here are the basic ones.

Standard Agility. This array consists of 15 to 22 obstacles. Included are tunnels, weave poles, and jumps, among others.

Jumping. As named, it consists mainly of jumps. However, in some competitions, you may see tunnels and weave poles with jumping array.

Power And Speed. If the dog can accomplish the tasks untimed (that's power) then he will be pre-qualified to enter the timed test (speed).

Juniors. This refers to the person or handler and not the puppy. If the owner is below 18, then this is the competition that he or she can enter in.

Teams. This could be composed of two dogs and two handlers or three dogs with three handlers. It is similar to a relay where a baton is passed from one team of handler and dog to the next team of handler and dog, who in turn, would complete a portion of the agility course.

Gamblers. This is for the professional or confident teams only. The first half is freestyle where it will be up to the handler to decide how to run the course and what is the order of the course. The biggest challenge in this array is the fact that the handler is physically distant from the dog. He or she will give the command in the assigned location, a bit far from the dog.

Snooker. This is mostly "jumps" with a color scheme. There are three jumps colored red and all three are numbered as 1. There are other jump obstacles numbered 2 to 7, which are not red in color. The numbers are also the equivalent score for each performed jump for red and non-red alike. The dog must jump through a red one first, then through a non-red, then red again, and so on. To get the score, just total all the numbers, which the dog was able to perform within the allotted time.

To sum it up:

Puppy agility training is truly beneficial to you and your puppy. At times, it could get frustrating and disappointing. However, when the training is finished and even when you have not actually joined a competition, all those frustrations and disappointments would be forgotten. The feeling of fulfillment would be worth all the time and effort spent on training. How much more if there is a medal or ribbon for winning in a competition, right?

Chapter 13 – The Final Step In Training Your Puppy: Making The Training A Lifestyle

In this chapter, you will learn:

1. What Is The Final Step In Training Your Puppy?
2. The Importance Of Doing The Final Step In Training
3. The General Guidelines Of The Final Step In Training
4. The Parameters Of The Final Training
5. The Steps To Make All The Learned Skills A Lifestyle

What Is The Final Step In Training Your Puppy?

You have come to the end of the training session of your puppy. Your puppy has undergone the basic until the advanced training. That is all very good but there is one last step to take. This is very important and oftentimes, this is overlooked or missed by most owners. You must not take this last step for granted since failing to do so may defeat the very purpose of your training in the first place.

What is this final step?

Some dog experts call it "Puppy Proofing The Training." Maybe, the term "proofing" has caused confusion among owners (hence most of them miss this), as there is puppy proofing which means to arrange the house or the surrounding of the puppy in such as way that it would be safe for the puppy. This is a different kind of proofing. This is actually foolproofing the training so that it becomes a lifestyle for the puppy. This last step would cause the training to be inculcated such that this now becomes the natural thing for him to do. It becomes the reflex. It is now the lifestyle.

The Importance Of Doing The Final Step In Training

Imagine your puppy has complete mastery of the cue "settle" when he is at home. If you will not do this last step to your puppy, the cue "settle" might totally be forgotten when he is outside. Why?

It is not because your puppy has poor memory retention. On the contrary, he is very smart. However, when he is outside, there is a higher level of distraction and temptation that even a well-trained puppy would be willing to be "not himself" for a fleeting second just to savor the moment.

A great example of this in humans is the marshmallow test. A child would be asked to sit with a marshmallow in front of him. He would be given an instruction not touch or eat the marshmallow after a designated period of time. Many children (and even adults) failed at that test. Why? The temptation was so strong that they could not resist — which means that the tendency to satisfy oneself immediately was not mastered. However, if this impulse were well-managed or well-controlled, then delaying gratification would be easy.

What is the purpose of this final step?

Your training should be deeply imbedded in your puppy that at all times, whatever the circumstance might be and wherever or whoever he may be with, he would still perform the commanded task. This will take precedence over your puppy's own desire and natural urges. This way, you are guaranteed safety (of your puppy, yourself, and other people) and preservation of all the puppy's learned skills and behavior.

Just like human beings, puppies can lose their learning in the absence of practice. For instance, there are many people who have taken a new language tutorial. Lack of practice and usage of this new skill has caused many of those people to forget all the lessons they have learned and after a couple of months, the only words that would be retained would perhaps be the basic ones such as "hello" and "goodbye." What they knew during the tutorial would be put to waste.

That could happen to your puppy. The basic lessons such as sit and stay could possibly be remembered until old age but the other advanced skills could be forgotten. That is, unless this last step in training is applied. It will maintain the learned behavior or skill whatever and whenever the situation may be and wherever the puppy may be. It guarantees retention of the skill and behavior regardless of the place, time, person, and circumstance.

The General Guidelines of the Final Step in Training

Here are some pointers to remember:

1. Customize your training. Each puppy is unique — hence, even the learning capability is not the same for each puppy. Study your puppy's genetic makeup and try to align your training based on his breed and personality.
2. Establish the comfort and safety of the puppy before, during, and after the training. Remember, if the

training would be accepted as fun and enjoyable for the puppy, he would learn faster and more willingly.

3. Start from easy to difficult. Do you recall your student years? Your teacher used to give you written exams that were easy to answer at first and then, when you got to the middle or last part of the exam, there would be difficult questions already. Do the same thing to your puppy. Practice from easy skills, progressing to the difficult ones.

4. Start adding distraction to the training from the least desirable to the most wanted distraction such as:

   a. Squeaky toy,
   b. Bouncing ball,
   c. Running around your dog, and
   d. Throwing treats to your puppy.

While training your puppy, do some of these distractions, expecting your puppy to remain focused on you and not on the distraction. Never use a distraction that would frighten your dog. Instead of learning, there is a higher chance that he would be traumatized by it.

5. Be patient and understanding. Even a very well-trained puppy could make mistakes. Do not be too hard on yourself and on your puppy. Practice good communication with your puppy.

6. Do the training as early as you can and as often as possible. Usually, this occurs in the third session (whether basic or advanced training). When the puppy has learned the skill, for example "sit," apply the last step to foolproof the training.

The Parameters Of The Final Training

You would know that you have achieved this final step when your dog would still follow your command with the following scenarios:

> - Increased distance between you and your puppy. The maximum is 30 feet. Your puppy should comply with the verbal command even if you were this far away from him.
> - The puppy should remain composed, calm, and obedient to you even if the distance of the "object of attraction" is near him. This could be a toy or another animal. He must have full control of natural urges, whether the object of his attraction is 10 or 5 feet away from him or is facing him.
> - Your puppy should react the same way wherever he may be — inside or outside the house, in a familiar or new surrounding.
> - Another consideration is the surface. The puppy should follow whether he is in a field, cemented ground, sand, or dirt. The surfaces where the object used for the training should be placed in different locations too just like chairs, tables, and bed, to name a few.
> - The skill would be performed whatever the circumstance is — for instance, whether you are in a mall or park or just inside the house; whether he is wearing a leash or not; or maybe, you are alone with him or in a crowd. Try out as many possible scenarios as possible.
> - The skill would be performed whatever your position is when you are giving the command. If you were lying

down (this would be useful when you are hurt or in an emergency) or standing up or sitting down, would he still comply? Try other positions you can think of.

➢ The dog would obey whatever the time is — whether morning or night.

➢ Try also to change your voice and observe for compliance of your puppy.

➢ The command is done even when you disappear after you gave the order. Say "sit" and then go out. Try to see if he remained seated while you were gone.

➢ Do it the other way around. The puppy obeys even when you disappear before you issue the command. For example, go out from the presence of your puppy first and then say "sit." Check whether he complied or not.

➢ Lastly, the puppy obeys even if there are no prompts and lures.

When you observe that your puppy can do the guidelines, it simply means that you have successfully achieved the last step.

The Steps To Make All The Learned Skills A Lifestyle

This is now the training part. So, how do you make your dog remember the skill and lessons for life? Simple. It is through repeated practice of the learned behavior or skill of the puppy, with varying degrees or levels of distractions, so that wherever the puppy may be, you can be sure that he would still do the mastered skill.

In this illustration, the "down" skill would be used all throughout the steps. It is assumed that your puppy has mastery of the "down" command already while inside the house. Here are the step-by-step techniques:

1. *Understand that your dog thinks differently from you* (or in general, from all human beings). Here is a good example. You were taught by your parents not to hit another person. You understand that this order covers not hitting your sibling, a stranger, your parents, classmates, and any human being for that matter. This principle does not apply to dogs. If you taught him to assume the "down" position while at home, it would not register that he should also obey the "down" cue when he is outside the home. Do not be surprised that he will not comply with the "down" cue when he is at the playground or park. You may get frustrated and think that your puppy is simply hardheaded but he is not. He just thinks differently. This is the reason for this last step. Your dog would learn to act the same way during training and during the actual situation (even if the conditions are different) because you would expose him to all possible situations.

2. Practice the "down" skill any time of the day. When he follows your order whenever you tell him to, he is ready for the next level.

3. Do the fading lures or prompts — meaning, the dog should obey the cue even when there are no rewards or treats after compliance.

4. Do the "down" cue and then begin to add a distraction. For example, have another favorite person enter the room while he is in a "down" position. Practice until he remains in that position. Try to make it more tempting to him. Ask another favorite family member to enter. You would know that he is ready for the next level when he remains in the down position even when another of his favorite persons comes in.

5. Add another distraction. For example, turn on the radio or television. Again, add some more distractions like having another pet inside the training area or children who are running around. Lastly, give him the distraction that he truly loves above all like a treat or a favorite toy.

6. When he is compliant even with all these distractions, it is time to change the location. Bring him to another training area, like the backyard. Time each session for 10 minutes each. Stay enthusiastic and upbeat about the training so that your puppy would feel the same. Find another more tempting location to do the skill when he can remain in that position while inside the backyard. Just in case he commits a mistake, simply go back to the last location where he was responsive to the command.

7. This time, go to the next parameter. Increase your distance from your puppy gradually. You are now training him to be obedient even when you are not so near. You can proceed to the next parameter when he follows even when you are 30 feet away.

8. Try to change your voice and see if he would still obey the command. Proceed to the next step when he does even with the use of various tones and dictions.

9. Give the command in different positions like while you are lying down on your tummy or while you are pretending to be asleep.

10. Give the command and leave the area. Come back and see if he complied. Do the opposite. Leave the area and give the command. Expect him to obey even though he cannot see you but only hear you.

By this time, the learned skill is now a part of his lifestyle. He would be compliant whatever the situation may be. Do these steps for all his learned skills. This may take some time but it would be worth it. There is so much to gain from a well-behaved puppy in whatever scenario he may be.

Chapter 14 – The Ultimate Guide To Puppy Health

In this chapter, you will learn:

1. Vaccination - The Preventive Care For Your Puppy
    a. The 4 Core Vaccines
    b. The Non-Core Vaccines
2. Know The Symptoms Of Different Dog Illnesses
3. Common Puppy Health Issues And Their Remedies
    a. Parasites
    b. Fleas
    c. Single-Cell Parasites
    d. Skin Mites
    e. Diarrhea
    f. Constipation

Health is wealth and this saying is applicable to your puppy, too. Maintain the good health of your puppy by giving him love, care, and protection the same way you would to yourself and your family. What is the best way to accomplish this? Prevention is always better than cure, really.

From day one of your puppy until his adult years, make sure that he is thoroughly checked by a veterinarian. Follow the vet's recommendations and advices. The first among these is about vaccination.

Vaccination - The Preventive Care For Your Puppy

Vaccinations are divided into Core and Non-Core. Core vaccines simply mean must-have vaccines. These are not optional. All puppies should be administered these vaccines.

Non-core vaccines, on the other hand, are optional and should be given on a case-to-case basis.

The 4 Core Vaccines:

- Canine Adenovirus-2 or CAV-2. It is also known as Canine Hepatitis. This is protection for the liver.
- Canine parvovirus or Parvo. This is protection from a viral disease that may affect the following organs of your puppy: intestines, bone marrow, lymph nodes, and even the heart.
- Distemper. This vaccine is another protection from a viral disease, which may affect your puppy's lungs, intestines, and brain.
- Rabies. This is protection for you, other people, and your puppy from a fatal viral disease affecting the central nervous system of the puppy.

The start of vaccination is usually at the 8th week of a puppy's life. Before this, puppies have natural immunity that they got from their mother. Take note that if you missed the vaccination and the puppy acquired the disease, there would be no cure for your puppy and he would die. These vaccinations can save your puppy's life and in some cases, even a person's life, including yours.

The Non-Core Vaccines:

Depending on your location and your puppy's activities (For example, does he travel and socialize a lot?), here are some non-core vaccines that he might benefit from.

- Corona Virus. It is a vaccine that will protect the puppy's intestine from a viral disease.
- Bordatella. This is protection from a respiratory bacterial disease more popularly known as Kennel Cough.

- Giardia. This is a vaccine against an internal parasitic disease.
- Lyme Disease. It is a vaccine that protects the puppy from a bacterial disease affecting the joints and other major organs.

Ask your veterinarian for the schedule of these shots as they may vary. Inquire about booster shots for older dogs.

Know The Symptoms Of Different Dog Illnesses

Some puppies may look well on the outside but they may be suffering from some illnesses internally. As the owner, you have to be very alert for the symptoms of different dog illnesses. Being observant may save the life of your puppy.

To do this, you must learn what a healthy puppy looks like. Here is a brief assessment of a healthy puppy from head to foot.

> ➢ A healthy puppy has a cool and moist nose. If you notice that your puppy is always sneezing or has a nasal discharge, it is safe to assume that he is of poor health.
> ➢ The gums should be pink. If the gums are pale, the puppy might be suffering from anemia.
> ➢ There should be no soft spot on the top of the head. This could be an open fontanel, which can be an indication of hydrocephalus.
> ➢ The puppy's eyes should be bright and clear. There should be no lines or white spots on the pupils of the eyes.
> ➢ The ears should not have any foul smell. If you notice that your dog is always shaking his head or cries

whenever you pat him near the ears, then there must be something wrong with his ears.

- Check the heart, too. The heartbeat should be regular and vibrant.
- Of course, the coat of the dog is a good way to determine his health. He should not have excessive scratching as this could suggest mites, fleas, or other skin disorders.
- Observe how he walks, too. There should no limping or faltering gait. He should also be happy and active. A dog that suddenly refuses to move even when he is offered his favorite toy or treat is obviously not well.
- Check his water and food intake as well. There should be no loss of appetite.

When in doubt, it is better to overreact than ignore or dismiss the signs. An hour could be too late for your puppy. Bring your puppy to his vet immediately and report the symptoms that you noticed.

The Common Puppy Health Issues and Their Remedies

Here are some of the health issues you may encounter with your puppy and their respective remedies.

Parasites

Most parasites would not cause so much damage on your puppy but if left untreated, they could harm your puppy really badly. Therefore, do not take it lightly when your puppy has fleas, mites, or intestinal worms. Take note, however, that parasites such as giardia protozoa, ticks, and heartworms could be fatal for them from day one.

Here are the different parasites that your puppy might have.

1. Intestinal Worms. They come in various shapes and sizes.
   a. Roundworms – These can be transmitted from the mommy dog to the puppies or through feces. You can see these parasites in the stool or sometimes, in the vomit of your puppy.
   b. Tapeworms – The seemingly not-so-harmful fleas are the reasons for the transmission of tapeworms to the puppy. You could also determine the presence of tapeworm by looking at your pup's feces. Eliminate this parasite by eliminating the fleas.
   c. Whipworms and Hookworms – These intestinal worms are found in the soil and feces. They can be transferred to humans so bring your pet to the vet immediately and have him treated.
   d. Heartworms – This is considered as the most dangerous among all intestinal worms. Mosquitoes are the culprits for the transmission of heartworms to the puppies.

Unfortunately, these intestinal worms can be transmitted to humans too, especially to children. Therefore, protect yourself and your family by being careful in the disposal of the waste of your sick puppy. Always practice strict hand-washing techniques. It is better if you would send your pet to the veterinarian as soon as possible rather than give him over-the-counter drugs.

Fleas

These parasites reside in the dog's fur and suck his blood. They can multiply really fast. Although they are not initially hazardous to your puppy's health, they can be if left untreated since they can proliferate really fast. Fleabites can also be very itchy and irritating for the puppy. As mentioned, they can also transmit tapeworms to the puppy.

There are many tick medications that you can apply to your puppy yourself (with the doctor's prescription and instructions). There are medicated collars that can prevent the occurrence of fleas, too. Here are some tips when treating your puppy for fleas.

> ➢ Do not use these medicines to nursing, pregnant, or sick dogs without informing your vet first.
> ➢ Follow the instructions on how to apply or administer the medicine. Take note of the age requirement before you give it to your puppy.
> ➢ Store the remaining medicines properly. Keep it out of reach from children and pets.
> ➢ Always practice hygiene and wash your hands properly for every contact that you have with the puppy.
> ➢ Do not allow other people, especially young children, to play or pet your dog while under medication. Keep him away from other pets as well.
> ➢ Observe your puppy for any untoward symptoms and send him immediately to the vet for treatment.

➢ Avoid re-infestation by treating your environment, the dog's things, furniture, and other items that have come in contact with your dog. You can ask for professional help or you can do this yourself — provided that you follow the guidelines on how to do those things carefully.

Single-Cell Parasites

Single-cell parasites are usually present in the intestines of the puppies; however, their natural immunities protect them from these parasites. Examples of these are coccidian and giardia. When the puppy's immune system is weakened (due to various reasons), these parasites can overwhelm the other systems and cause the puppy to be severely sick.

The puppy may manifest the following symptoms: diarrhea, loss of appetite, lethargy, vomiting, and weight loss. Take note that these symptoms are all potentially fatal to your puppy. Refer your puppy to the vet immediately for treatment and management.

Skin Mites

Unlike fleas, these parasites cannot be seen by the naked eye. These parasites also reside in your puppy's ears most of the time. One type of this mite, known as Sarcoptes mite, more popularly known as scabies, can be transferred to humans.

The vet may prescribe oral meds as well as medicated shampoo to treat this problem. Make sure that you wear gloves and follow strict hand-washing techniques every time you handle the affected puppy as you can acquire these mites, too.

Diarrhea

Diarrhea can occur quite often and most of the time, there is no cause for alarm when it happens. However, do not take it lightly. Always monitor your puppy closely especially if the diarrhea is accompanied by vomiting. He might suffer from dehydration and that could be fatal.

Causes of diarrhea:

1. Eating things other than his food. It's natural for a puppy to be curious and try to eat anything he sees on the ground. This may include flowers, papers, trash, insects, and even rodents sometimes. Hence, diarrhea is common among dogs. You can prevent this when your puppy has mastered the "leave it" skill. If the puppy has not learned this skill, give him probiotic supplements that can strengthen his digestive system.
2. Infections and illnesses. Very young puppies have immature or underdeveloped immune systems — therefore, they are very prone to diseases, especially those that are contagious. Side effects of these illnesses include stomach upset and diarrhea. Avoid this by completing his vaccines and taking good care of your puppy.
3. Worms and other parasites of the intestine. In some instances, the puppies were born with these parasites. Otherwise, they acquired these parasites during their growing up days. Vaccinations would be helpful here, too.
4. Change in diet. This is very common. Most of the time, this is self-limiting, meaning that it would heal by itself.

The stomach would adjust to the new food and diarrhea would stop. Just introduce the new diet gradually.

5. Stress. Unknown to many people, dogs have many stressors. Examples are traveling, having new pets with them, living with new owners, or being in a new location, to name just a few. These things could weaken the puppy's immune system and allow parasites to flourish and harm them. If possible, avoid exposing stressful things to your puppy. However, if it cannot be helped, reinforce comfort and peace to your puppy by showering him with love and affection.

Constipation

Among the common health issues of puppies, this one is the least dangerous. Constipation can be caused by:

- ➢ Inadequate water intake
- ➢ Lack of exercise and movement
- ➢ Stress (like being in a new home or new owner)
- ➢ Hairballs (This can happen to dogs who like to lick themselves.)
- ➢ Eating things they should not be eating like plastic, trash, toys, rubber, and wood
- ➢ Medications. Constipation can be a side effect of a medication that your puppy might be taking.

Note: If your puppy is showing symptoms of distress, pain, and/or a bloated or distended abdomen, bring him to the vet immediately. He may require surgery.

Here are some home remedies for your puppy's constipation:

Puppy Training Guide 4th Edition

1. Add bran to his diet. This is high in fiber and can help loosen his bowel.
2. Increase his fluid intake.
3. Always take your dog for a walk. This is his exercise and it can help improve his defecation.
4. Add oil. A little oil in the diet can soften his stool and act as lubricant for the easy passage of stool.
5. Give him special dog food. Ask your local pet shops for special dog food designed to treat the constipation of your puppy.
6. Administer over-the-counter drugs. You can also administer OTC drugs to relieve the constipation of your puppy. Do not make a habit of doing this though.

Make the health of your puppy a priority.

Chapter 15 – The Ultimate Guide To Puppy-Proofing Your Home

In this chapter, you will learn:

1. How To Puppy-Proof The Inside Of Your House
   a. Kitchen
   b. Bedroom
   c. Bathroom
   d. Living Room
   e. Home Office
2. How To Puppy-Proof The Outside Of Your House
   a. Garage
   b. Backyard

Dogs are naturally curious. They love to explore and taste and eat everything they see. The old saying, "Curiosity killed the cat" should actually be changed to "Curiosity killed the dog" as there are many instances wherein these pets were killed due to their natural love to discover new things.

The best way to prevent any untoward incident from happening to your dog because of curiosity is to puppy-proof your home. This is one way of maintaining the health of your puppy. This is quite simple to do, actually. This is similar to proofing your house for your toddler or child.

How To Puppy-Proof The Inside Of Your House

There is nothing that will escape your dog so make sure that you puppy-proof all areas.

Kitchen

Puppy Training Guide 4th Edition

This is where you usually keep your food. This is also one of the favorite places of your puppy. Some people think that if these "people food" are safe for them then they are also safe for dogs. Nothing can be further from the truth. Be aware of the following foods that may cause the very life of your puppy. Here is a list:

a. Avocados. This means not only the fruit but also the leaves, bark, and seed. These fruits contain persin which is found to be toxic for dogs.
b. All alcoholic beverages. Alcohol can damage the liver of the puppy especially if the puppy is small and young.
c. Onions and garlic. Whatever the preparation of onions and garlic (powder, raw, dehydrated, or cooked), these two can destroy the red blood cells of the puppy and cause anemia.
d. Caffeine. Anything with caffeine like chocolates, coffee, tea, colas, and some energy drinks can be fatal to puppies. There is no antidote for this so beware.
e. Grapes and raisins. Who would have thought that these could damage the kidneys of your puppy and cause his death? They can and so, make sure that there is no way that your dog can have access to these fruits.
f. Milk and dairy products. You see people feeding their dogs with ice cream during summer. This is a really bad decision. Milk and dairy products can cause diarrhea, leading to the dehydration of your puppy.
g. Macadamia nuts. Do you know that it only takes 6 pieces of macadamia nuts to kill a puppy? A faster death can take place if your puppy consumed a chocolate with macadamia nuts.

h. Food with xylitol. Xylitol can be found in candies, gums, pastries, and diet food. They can disrupt the endocrine system of the puppy and cause hypoglycemia, which could also lead to liver failure and afterward, death.

i. Raw eggs. They can acquire bacteria there like salmonella and E. coli.

j. Raw meat and fish. Sometimes, intestinal worms originate from these. Properly cook them before you give them to your puppy.

k. Your medicine. Heart medicines can be fatal to your dogs.

Have the number of your vet pinned near the phone or posted on the ref in case your dog swallowed something toxic for him. Plus, always have the contact number of ASPCA or the Animal Poison Control Center within your reach.

Bathroom

Another dangerous place for your puppy is the bathroom. Usually, you would find the cleansing agents under the sink. Lock these cabinets and secure all toxic agents from your pets.

Big dogs love to drink and explore the toilet bowl, too. Keep them safe from drowning and acquiring harmful bacteria by keeping the toilet seat down all the time. Plus, your puppy can be hurt from razors and other sharp items that can be found in the bathroom — not to mention that shampoos, soaps, and other toiletries can be hazardous to your puppy's health so place them where your puppy would not be able to reach them.

Put a trash bin with a locking lid in the bathroom since your puppy loves to dig into trash cans, too.

Bedroom

The bedroom may seem safe enough for your puppy. However, your puppy might ingest small items like coins, hair ties, pieces of jewelry, and other inedible items. Remove also the cords and wires that can strangle your puppy. Keep the clutter away so that there is no danger of your puppy consuming things he should not.

Living Room

Cords and other things that may strangle your puppy abound in the living room. Plus, other items such as magazines, shoes, gadgets, and decorative plants (which can be toxic to your puppy) are usually found in this area. Keep these out of reach from your puppy.

Home Office

Some people convert a room as an office. In here, you would find paper clips, staple wires, scissors, letter openers, and other office supplies that may hurt your puppy. Soft items like rubber bands can be chewed and swallowed and cause blockage in the stomach. Again, always close the door leading to this room or protect your puppy by placing these items where he cannot reach them.

How To Puppy-Proof The Outside Of Your House

If you think there are many items to hide inside the house to protect your puppy, the same can be said in puppy-proofing the outside of your house.

Garage

The garage is where you usually store not only your cars, but also most of your chemicals. This is one of the most dangerous places for your puppy. It is in here that you would find the following items:

- Cleaners
- Insecticides
- Paint
- Rat and Rodent Poison
- Fertilizers
- Gasoline
- Antifreeze (It is fatal if even a small amount were ingested.)

Sharp objects and heavy equipment also abound here — all which can hurt your playful puppy when they intentionally or unintentionally touch them. Therefore, you need to secure all these items in containers or boxes and place them where your puppy would not be able to get a hold of them.

Backyard

Plants

Puppies love the backyard for this is the equivalent of a playground for them. What could possibly harm your puppy in the backyard? A lot. Some plants, which are safe for people, can be poisonous for your puppy. Examples are bird-of-paradise, avocado, onion, garlic, lupine, foxglove, and daffodils which can cause various harmful reactions when ingested by your puppy.

There are at least 700 plants that can be dangerous to your puppy. Here is a list of the common plants that may be in your backyard, aside from the aforementioned.

> ➢ Lilies
> ➢ Tulips
> ➢ Azalea
> ➢ Oleander
> ➢ Yew
> ➢ Iris
> ➢ Mustards
> ➢ Potato
> ➢ Wild radish

Fence

Your fence is designed to protect you and your family. However, it could be a cause of harm for your puppy. Here are some things you can do to ensure the safety of your puppy.

1. Your fence should at least be 6 feet if your dog is big or medium-built. Your puppy could jump over it and hurt himself.
2. Check the parameters of your fence for any holes or openings where he would be able to squeeze or wiggle out.
3. Fences with decorative sharp irons can injure your puppy when they try to jump over it.
4. Dogs love to dig. Protect them from this instinct by placing stones along the fence so they would not be able to dig that part and get out of your backyard.

Other Things

There might be cables, wires, and garden hoses lying around the backyard. Remove them as your puppy might get entangled in them or they might chew these and they may suffer from various digestive system medical conditions.

A swimming pool can also be a danger zone for the puppy as he can fall in it and drown. You can put a gate before the pool.

Safety First

Prior to bringing your puppy home, check all these things first. Continually check the house inside and outside for other things you might have missed or overlooked. Always be on the lookout for the safety of your puppy.

Chapter 16 - How to Show Love and Affection to Your Puppy

Puppies by nature are quite affectionate. They aren't referred to as man's best friends for nothing. Puppies will patiently wait for you at home while you are out working in the office or at school, or out partying with your friends on a weekend night. They will warmly welcome you home when you return tired, they will jump up and down in their excitement to see you, and lick your face simply because they missed you while you were gone.

Puppies are also loyal. They will stand by you no matter what and protect you when they feel possible threats directed towards you. Puppies are like infants, as already mentioned many times in this book, for you to understand that at a certain point in your life that you live with puppies in the house, they will cease to be mere animals and become friends, and family. And that having been said, like any relationship you have with any human person, puppies are also capable of loving. They love their masters most of all. They will try their best to learn new tricks to amuse you because they delight in the sight of your smile, knowing with their instincts that their master is pleased with them.

Like your human friends and family, puppies also get hurt; and their feelings also matter. You have your family, coworkers, classmates, and friends to spend the whole day with. You may have a lover, or any close family member, but your puppy only has you. This is why your puppy is fond of you, and sometimes you don't realize that they expect a certain amount of love back from you. Having a pet is having a responsibility. Animals have lives too, and you ought to respect that, especially since you chose to have and take care of one.

In that regard, this chapter will tell you the ways through which you can show your love and affection for your puppy by expounding on the following points of discussion:

- o Talk to your puppy.
- o Don't hug your puppy all the time.
- o Go on dates and take them for a walk.
- o Scratch your puppy.
- o Play with your puppy.
- o Feed your puppy well.
- o Clean your puppy.
- o Introduce your puppy to every member of your family.
- o Spend time with your puppy (no matter how busy you are).
- o Just love them. Period.

Talk to your puppy.

It is of course both surreal and absurd to talk to someone who will not respond to what you are saying, or not in your language, at least. Puppies may not understand what you are specifically telling them, but they can feel that you are confiding in them when you talk with them. Puppies are sensitive, not just of their own feelings, but of yours as their master, most of all.

Puppies may not understand you verbally and respond to you in the same way, but animals rely on body language and gestures for communication. Aside from this, dogs are great at sensing situations. There are puppy owners who testify that they strongly believe their puppies understand them. When for example, a puppy owner is crying and she talks to her puppy about her problems without really expecting anything from her animal friend, her puppy would come to her side and lick her face. This is a puppy's way of reassuring you that despite the language barrier between the two of you, he/she is listening and he/she is there for you.

Your puppy will recognize your praising tone, commanding tone, and corrective tone. Since the sadness in your voice when you talk to your puppy is none of those three, it will send a signal to your puppy that the situation is not part of a system or a routine that you both has come to practice during trainings and your daily activities together. Talking to your puppy can also do you well, just to let the emotions out there, onto someone who won't tell anyone your secrets—of course.

Don't hug your puppy all the time.

This can be a crucial topic. Some puppies like being hugged and some don't. There are some dogs who feel restrained when humans hug them all the time, especially human persons that are strangers to them. Animals communicate differently in a lot of ways from humans. For instance, in the human world, a hug is an important display of affection, and it has a number of degrees: a supportive hug, a comforting hug, a greeting hug, an "I love you" hug, etc. However, it might be different for your puppy's world.

Puppies may feel like their private or personal space is being invaded too often, and the chances are they will become territorial and refuse to react with tolerance of the situation, which may result in them barking at you or those around them. And in certain situations wherein too much hugging frustrates them, they tend to bite their offender. As much as it is understandable for humans to want to hug your puppy because they find him cute and fluffy, you may show your affection for your puppy in ways that will not necessarily irritate him and cause bad habits and unwanted scenarios to happen.

It is also worth explaining that although this is very common among puppies and dogs alike, there are some case wherein they grow fond of physical affection such as hugging and kissing them, especially if the puppy was born in your house and grew up with the knowledge that hugging is actually normal. It is still practically wise to observe your puppy's reaction to your displays of affection. If, for example, your dog or puppy yawns and turns his/her face away from you when you hug him/her, it is most likely that they tolerate your human ways, but they are not exactly delighted with such behavior. Try minimizing your affectionate ways that involve restraining or confining them.

Go on dates and take them for a walk.

As much as the need to cage your pet sometimes

arrives, don't love them when they're new and then lock them up and let them rot in there until they die. Puppies would love to spend time with you, and that in itself could bring you great joys that can only be acquired by having a puppy. Give yourself the chance to get to know your animal companion. Befriend your puppy. Go on dates to the park and play fetch. Set a time and day for walking your puppy around the neighborhood. It not only exercises both of you physically, but it also practices the strength of your bond.

Puppies like being given the chance to explore, provided that they know you are there to protect them, just as they are ready to protect you from any harm that you may encounter along the way. Walking your dog or your puppy also prepares him/her for situations like when you need to bring him/her to a gathering; because he/she will have the chance to meet other people and other dogs along the street, your puppy will be trained for socializing without being threatened that other people or other animals are always out to get him/her.

Spending some quality time in the streets or by the park also promotes trust, because your puppy would know that he/she can explore around and still be assured that you will be waiting right where you were. It promotes trust because he/she will feel that you are in this adventure together, looking out for each other as you cross the street or do any other activity.

Scratch your puppy.

When you come home and your puppy knows nothing about you not having been with him/her all day, your puppy will most probably jump on you and place his/her head on your lap. Scratch your puppy. This is your puppy's way of telling you that he/she missed you. Your puppy is trying to find out where you have been and who you were with by sniffing you.

Puppies love lying on their backs and being scratched on their tummies. When you massage them, you are also massaging them in a way, and puppies need that—not just to feel that you are affectionate toward them but it is also helpful in strengthening their bones. Puppies like the attention their human companions give them, and scratching and massaging them is one of the best ways of making them feel that you love them.

 Play with your puppy.

Puppies long for the breeze of air to stir their hair. They have a desire they are yet to realize for wide open fields where they can run freely but never too far so as not to lose sight of you. Puppies like to play, just like the kids in every home do. So let them play, and play with them. This exercises their body and is also healthy for their minds and hearts because they receive a signal from you that you are having fun with them and that you are enjoying their company.

Feed your puppy well.

Puppies also know that you care for them through the food that you prepare for them. Put some effort into the simple dog food that you usually feed your puppy. They will recognize this attempt at making them more welcome at home. Like men, experts say that the way to a dog's heart is through their stomachs. Also remember the old proverb that goes, "A dog is loyal to the hands that feed it."

Clean your puppy.

It is simple, really. Nobody wants to show affection to a puppy (or any animal for that matter) that is unclean. Cleaning your puppy like giving him/her a shower can also be a fun way to spend time together. Making sure that your puppy's hygiene is cared for is your responsibility as his/her master. This shows puppies that you love them because they associate the feeling of being clean with the affectionate gestures that often come afterward: a scratch behind his/her ear, a loving pat on the head, and a quick hug.

Making sure that your puppy is clean, as well as his/her personal space, is also to take care of your puppy's health. By doing so, you are also taking care of your family's health because you are preventing the bacteria that may come from your puppy's lack of hygiene to enter and spread into your home. Remember that at this point in time, your puppy has now become a legitimate member of your family and he/she deserves to be treated like one since the day you decided to have a pet puppy.

Introduce your puppy to every member of the family.

For both your family and your puppy's safety and well-being, you must introduce your pet puppy to the rest of the members of the family.
Doing so will take away your puppy's notion that your family is posing a threat upon him/her, because they are still strangers to your puppy's eyes. Once you have made it clear that your puppy is safe in your home in the presence of other people aside from yourself, you erase the possibility of your puppy either being traumatized by the small crowd or throwing a tantrum at one of your family members which may result in physical harm.

This is also effective in welcoming your pet puppy to the family. This is a way of saying that your puppy is one you now, that he/she is also part of the family. Once this has been done, your puppy will lose the intimidation of sitting next to your younger brother, or licking your father's hand. Your puppy will feel comfortable and at ease lying down on the floor with your cousins during your family's movie night and other similar get-togethers. The point is to make your puppy feel that he/she belongs to your home.

Spend time with your puppy no matter how busy you are.

No matter how busy you are, find the time to at least pat your puppy's head when you come home from work or school; even just a brief tummy scratch or a kiss on his /her forehead before going to bed will do. When your puppy shows signs that he/she wants to spend time with you but you are too busy or too tired at the moment, dismiss the request politely and tell your puppy that you will spend time with him/her for the rest of the day.

Puppies are like children. They will feel bad when their dad won't play ball at the yard with them because dad is busy working on something; and like a child, a puppy will hold on to your word when you say that you will play with him/her sometime within that week. Do not bring your puppy's hopes down. See to it that you fulfill this promise, even if it is just a five-minute game of Frisbee fetching. Otherwise, they might lose trust in you (but they will love you regardless).

Just love them. Period.

Lastly, just love your puppies the way you would love any other thing. Value them because they have lives, and especially because they value you a lot. Love them because they are the only ones who will still lick your face even though you have left them all day without saying goodbye. Love them because you are all they have. Love them because on days when not even ice cream or hanging out with your friends could cheer you up, they will still try. Love them because they will never leave, unless you ask them to. Love them, simply because they deserve it. And because you deserve their love too.

Conclusion

Thank you again for purchasing this book, *"Puppy Training Guide: The Ultimate handbook to train your puppy in obedience, crate training and potty training"*!

Truly, caring for a puppy is a huge but very rewarding experience. The reason is that you have to carefully plan on how to properly train your puppy when it comes to obedience, crate and potty. In fact, training your puppy will require a great deal of effort, time and money by every member in the household. Therefore, training a puppy is much like a group project. The objective of course, is to train the puppy well so that he or she will become a well-mannered, well-behaved and fun-loving adult dog.

I hope this book was able to help you to fully understand the fundamentals of obedience training, crate training and potty training. It is fervently hoped by the author that this would be a big help to struggling puppy owners out there.

Finally, if you enjoyed this book, please take the time to share your thoughts and post a review on Amazon. We do our best to reach out to readers and provide the best value we can. Your positive review will help us achieve that. It'd be greatly appreciated!

Thank you and good luck!